THE BASICS

Food Ethics: The Basics is a concise yet comprehensive introduction to the ethical dimensions of the production and consumption of food. It offers an impartial exploration of the most prominent ethical questions relating to food and agriculture including:

- Should we eat animals?
- Are locally produced foods ethically superior to globally sourced foods?
- Do people in affluent nations have a responsibility to help reduce global hunger?
- Should we embrace bioengineered foods?
- What should the role of government be in promoting food safety and public health?

Using extensive data and real world examples, as well as providing suggestions for further reading, *Food Ethics: The Basics* is an ideal introduction for anyone interested in the ethics of food.

Ronald L. Sandler is Professor of Philosophy and Director of the Ethics Institute at Northeastern University.

The Basics

FOOD ETHICS

THE BASICS

Ronald L. Sandler

Routledge
Taylor & Francis Group

LONDON AND NEW YORK

First published 2015
by Routledge
2 Park Square, Milton Park, Abingdon, Oxon OX14 4RN

and by Routledge
711 Third Avenue, New York, NY 10017

Routledge is an imprint of the Taylor & Francis Group, an informa business

British Library Cataloguing in Publication Data
A catalogue record for this book is available from the British Library

Library of Congress Cataloging-in-Publication Data
Sandler, Ronald L.
Food ethics : the basics / Ronald Sandler. – 1 [edition].
pages cm. – (The basics)
Includes bibliographical references.
1. Food–Moral and ethical aspects. 2. Food industry and trade–Moral and ethical aspects. 3. Agriculture–Moral and ethical aspects. 4. Diet–Moral and ethical aspects. I. Title.
TX357.S265 2014
178–dc23
2014031916

ISBN: 978-0-415-83643-2 (hbk)
ISBN: 978-0-415-83644-9 (pbk)
ISBN: 978-0-203-69440-4 (ebk)

Typeset in Bembo
by Taylor and Francis Books

To Karen G. Sandler

CONTENTS

ACKNOWLEDGMENTS

This book developed from two courses that I teach at Northeastern University: Food in Contemporary Context and Food Ethics. I am grateful to the students that I have had in those courses for sharing with me their questions, experiences, perspectives and knowledge about food and agriculture. I am fortunate to teach such engaged, thoughtful and capable students, and I suspect that I learn much more from them than they do from me.

I am deeply indebted to Christopher Bosso, with whom I co-teach Food in Contemporary Context, for dramatically improving my understanding of the political and regulatory dimensions of food issues, as well as for providing comments on a complete draft of this manuscript. His fingerprints are all over the development of my thinking about food systems (and so all over this book). John Basl also provided extensive comments on this manuscript, especially the chapters on animals and bioengineering, which are much improved as a result of his many constructive criticisms and suggestions.

Jodie Ly provided valuable research assistance on this project with respect to fact checking, tracking down sources, organizing references, and preparing the manuscript for publication. She also gave me excellent advice regarding readability—passages that needed to be written more clearly, as well as terminology and ideas that required further explication. I am thankful for her hard work and patience with me throughout the writing and revising process.

I also thank all the people at Routledge who supported this project and contributed to the production process: Andy Humphries, Siobhan Poole, Iram Satti, Michael Helfield, and Andrew Watts. From my perspective, it could not have gone more smoothly from beginning to end.

Most of all, I thank my family, particularly my wife, Emily, and children, Elijah and Ruth. This book is dedicated to my mother, Karen Sandler. Thanks for everything, Mom. Your generosity and selflessness never cease to astound me, and you make the world's best mandel bread.

INTRODUCTION

WHY FOOD ETHICS?

Food is important. One reason, of course, is that we need it to survive and thrive. But more than that, it is part of the fabric of our lives. We structure our days around food. We socialize around food. We celebrate with food. Our identities are expressed through food. We enjoy food. Food can be deeply personal and cultural.

Food is also global. Crop and animal agriculture occupy over a third of the Earth's land. Over a billion people work in agriculture (approximately 35% of all workers), and hundreds of millions more work in food-related industries. After oil, crops and animals are the most traded commodities in the world. Each year, 56 billion land animals and 90 billion marine animals are killed for human consumption.

It is no surprise, then, that food is contested. There are controversies over what we should eat. There are controversies over where our food should come from. There are controversies over how our food should be grown. There are controversies over food technologies. There are controversies regarding food distribution. There are controversies regarding food policies. As the term is used in this book, a *food issue* is any contested aspect of the life cycle of food: agriculture and capture, processing, manufacture, distribution, transportation, preparation, consumption and disposal. Food issues concern the agro-food systems that we are part of, as well as our individual food choices.

Food issues and choices are very often ethical issues and choices. They concern rights, justice, power, autonomy, control, sustainability, animal welfare and human well-being. The claims that people make about them are *prescriptive*—they are about what we *should* do, as well as about which food systems and policies we *should* support. Should we eat animals? Should we eat local? Should we embrace genetically modified crops? Should we help address global malnutrition? As a result, they involve views about what matters, what has value, what principles we should live by, and what ideals we should strive for. We cannot make good choices about food consumption, food policy or food systems without attending to food ethics.

This book is an introduction to food ethics. It identifies the ethical components of food issues and elucidates the prominent ethical dimensions of food choices. The aim is to be informative, not to tell the reader what to do. Food choices are ultimately personal—everyone decides for themselves what they eat, where they shop, and what their politics are. For those who are interested in sorting out the ethics of their food-related practices, perhaps this book can help them to do so.

STRUCTURE AND APPROACH

Each chapter in this book focuses on a different topic area: food systems; food security; eating animals; bioengineering; food and health; and food and culture. Ethical analysis requires having a clear understanding of the issues being discussed. Therefore, each chapter contains (and often begins with) an extensive amount of background information—e.g. regarding relevant policies, empirical data and scientific research. After clarifying an issue, I highlight its ethical dimensions and identify the key values and ethical questions involved. In many cases, I then present the most prominent views and arguments regarding what ought to be done in response to it. Although my aim is not to defend any particular answer to any ethical question discussed, I do frequently identify what ethicists regard as the most promising views on an issue, indicate when a view or argument has widely recognized flaws, and suggest questions or perspectives that might be helpful for thinking through an issue.

The chapters are largely stand alone and can be read in any order. However, there are internal references that make connections across the topics discussed, and they sometimes refer the reader to a section in another chapter where there is a more comprehensive discussion of an issue or question. Moreover, a great many food issues concern or arise from aspects of the food systems in which we participate. Because the discourse around food systems is crucial context for understanding so many food issues, I recommend reading the chapter on food systems first (Chapter 1) if you are not already familiar with the food system debates.

Finally, I should mention one thing about what this book is not. It is not a study or a review of historical or cultural practices around food and agriculture, either in general or regarding particular traditions. Although the ethical significance of cultural and social context is frequently discussed (and Chapter 6 focuses on it), this book is in no way intended to be a book about *foodways*—i.e. the development, content and meaning of the distinctive agricultural and food-related practices of peoples. Sociological, historical, anthropological and cultural studies of food and agriculture are fascinating and valuable, but they are not the focus here.

FOOD SYSTEMS

Quite a lot of food issues emerge where our personal preferences, choices and practices intersect with broader social and ecological considerations, such as sustainability, biodiversity, human rights, global justice and animal welfare. What connects individual choices to the broader issues are the food systems in which we participate. *Food system* refers to the complex network of processes, infrastructures and actors that produce the food we eat and deliver it to where we eat it. Most of the food movements that we hear about—slow foods, local foods, organic foods and food justice—have emerged as a response to ethical concerns regarding the increasingly dominant food system often referred to as the *global food system*. This chapter presents the discourse around the global food system and the alternatives to it that have been proposed: local and regional systems. Not only are the controversies regarding food systems important in their own right, they also form the crucial backdrop against which other prominent ethical issues regarding food and agriculture play out.

WHAT IS THE GLOBAL FOOD SYSTEM?

Every food system involves agricultural production (e.g. crops and livestock) or capture (e.g. fishing), processing (e.g. slaughtering, refining, pressing and freezing), preparation (e.g. in manufacturing facilities, restaurants and homes), consumption and waste disposal. They all involve transportation, distribution, agricultural and processing supplies, technology, and exchange (or trade). What is distinctive about the global food system is that the food production and delivery networks are *transnational* and *industrial*. The global food system is decentralized and dynamic. There is no organized planning process, and the networks, actors, processes, policies and infrastructures that constitute it are constantly changing in response to numerous factors, such as technological innovation, consumer demand, economic conditions, weather patterns, regulations and geopolitical events. However, the transnational and industrial character of the system, which prioritizes efficiency, cost minimization and market success, favors the following features, several of which are central to the ethical discourse surrounding it. These features are not unique to the global food system, but are common across global industrial production and delivery systems.

- *Global sourcing*—Materials, labor and processing are sourced wherever they are least expensive.
- *Economies of scale*—Consolidation, vertical integration and large-scale production (at all levels—e.g. agriculture, processing and manufacturing) are favored because they increase coordination and reduce cost per unit of production.
- *Large actors*—The primary (or most influential) actors involved are corporations, international institutions and national governments due to their economic significance and ability to act globally and influence or set policy.
- *Mechanization and innovation*—Mechanization and novel technologies and processes are readily adopted if they can increase efficiency and lower cost.
- *Standardization*—Standardization of inputs (e.g. commodities and animals) and processes (e.g. manufacturing and preparation) along the supply chain increases production efficiency and allows for ready substitution (e.g. sourcing from different locations and replacing workers).
- *Commodification*—All elements of the system are valued (primarily or exclusively) in terms of their economic usefulness and are treated as fungible (able to be traded for money or another commodity) and substitutable.

- *Cost externalization*—Reducing consumer price and increasing profits incentivizes trying to pass on the costs (e.g. ecological, social or public health) of production processes to others or to society as a whole.
- *High-input needs (and capital costs)*—Intensive, large-scale production and global distribution require high levels of material inputs—e.g. fertilizer for agriculture, machinery for processing, and fossil fuels for transportation.

The quintessential illustration of the global industrial food system and the complexity of the global food chain is the fast food restaurant cheeseburger. It is inexpensive, sold around the world by large corporations, the same at every location, thoroughly processed, immediately available, anonymously produced and globally sourced. The fast food cheeseburger may be among the more industrial and global food items, but it is by no means an exception. Particularly for those of us in affluent nations, the food in our restaurants, on the shelves in our grocery stores, and in our homes is increasingly global, processed and ready for consumption.

ARGUMENTS FOR THE GLOBAL FOOD SYSTEM

The global food system is the result of globalization and industrialization applied to food and agriculture. Economic, technological and sociological factors have encouraged its development. These factors include the capacity to store and transport foodstuffs, the ability to communicate quickly and easily over long distances, the migration of people (and their culinary preferences and practices), and the development of international commodities markets. However, it was not inevitable that food systems would evolve in this way. There have been national and international policies to encourage it—e.g. free trade agreements to facilitate the movement of goods and services across borders, agricultural subsidies to dramatically increase production of commodity crops (e.g. corn and soybeans), patent laws that empower large actors (e.g. transnational agricultural supply companies), and concerted efforts (e.g. by international lenders and colonial powers) to move nations toward global commodity agriculture and away from locally consumed polyculture. (*Polyculture* refers to the practice of growing a large variety of edible plants;

commodity monoculture refers to the practice of growing large amounts of one type of crop for market sale.) Several arguments have been made in support of promoting a global industrial food system.

ARGUMENT FROM FEEDING THE WORLD

One of the primary arguments offered in support of the global food system is that we need it to meet the challenge of feeding everyone in the world. There are currently 7.2 billion people on the planet, and global population is expected to continue to increase in the coming decades. How many people there will be depends upon future fertility rates, which are measured in terms of the number of children born per woman. It is not possible to know precisely what those rates will be, so future population must be discussed in terms of scenarios. According to United Nations projections, if by the middle of this century the fertility rate drops to 2.24 children/woman, global population will be approximately 9.6 billion in 2050 and 10.9 billion by 2100. If the fertility rate is 2.74 children/woman, the projected population is 10.9 billion in 2050 and 16.6 billion in 2100. If the rate plummets to 1.74 children/woman, the population is projected to be only 8.3 billion by mid-century and 6.8 billion by 2100 (UN, 2013a).

There are good reasons to believe that the medium (or lower) fertility variant can be accomplished. Rates have been dropping all over the world, and there are policies that can effectively reduce them further. (These will be discussed in the next chapter.) Still, feeding a population of 7.2 billion people and growing is an enormous challenge. There are currently 842 million under-nourished people in the world, and it is estimated that global crop demand will increase between 60% and 120% by 2050, depending on factors such as population growth, economic growth and shifts in diets (Cassidy et al., 2013; Alexandratos and Bruinsma, 2012).

Feeding the world is a challenge that we must meet with finite natural resources. According to the United Nations Food and Agricultural Organization (FAO), approximately 38% of the Earth's surface is already used in food production (crop and pasture) (FAOSTAT, 2014a). India uses 60% of its land for agriculture, while the United States uses 45% (World Bank, 2014a). These rates have been relatively steady over many years, even as population has increased. The reason for this is that most land well suited to agriculture and not vital for other purposes is already under some form of agricultural use. (The only substantial areas for potential increase are forested regions in parts of Africa and South America.) Because the amount of land used in agriculture has remained steady, while population has increased, the amount of agricultural land used per person has been steadily dropping. Moreover, recent research suggests that there is an overall planetary limit to how much plant matter can grow in a year, crop or otherwise, based on such things as land availability, solar radiation and precipitation (Running, 2012). Thus, any additional plant resources we use for ourselves will diminish what is available for other species. It is already estimated that humans appropriate approximately 25% of biospheric or net primary plant production (Haberl et al., 2007; Krausmann et al., 2013). The situation is similar with respect to the oceans. Less than 13% of global fisheries are currently under-exploited. The rest are fully exploited (approximately 57%) or overexploited (approximately 30%). There is not much more production to be gotten from the sea, particularly if we are to leave sufficient resources for other species (FAO, 2012a).

Given that the amount of agricultural land in use per person has been declining, one might expect that the amount of calories produced and available per person has also been dropping. However, this is not the case: "In recent decades, the productivity potential of global agriculture has exceeded population growth, resulting in a steady, albeit slow, increase in average per capita food availability. For the world as a whole, per capita food supply rose from about 2,200 kcal/day in the early 1960s to more than 2,800 kcal/day by 2009 ... Protein and fat supplies, measured in grams per person per day, have also increased over the past ten years, with fat supply outpacing proteins" (FAOSTAT, 2013, p. 126). Globally, and in every major region, including Africa, Asia, Latin America and Oceania, more calories, fat and protein are produced and available in the food supply *per capita* today than in 1960, 1990 or 2000 (FAOSTAT, 2013; FAO, 2013c). Proponents of the global food system argue that this is the result of technological innovation and industrial efficiency, which have been spreading through the agriculture and food sectors over that time. The way to get more calories out of less land is to intensify production, to innovate and adopt new agricultural technologies, to add inputs (e.g. synthetic nitrogen fertilizer) as needed, to specialize production to what is best suited for a region (and then trade globally), to reduce crop loss (e.g. to pests and spoilage), to eliminate waste in the supply chain, and to deliver food when and where it is needed all over the world.

Increased production through industrialization is applied to animal agriculture as much as to crop agriculture. For example, in the United States, per cow milk production increased from 9,700 pounds/year to over 21,700 pounds/year between 1970 and 2012 due to improvements in milking technologies, feeds, breeds and hormones, as well as concentrated specialization (USDA-NASS, 2014; USDA, 2012b).

One core argument for the global food system, then, is that innovation, globalization, industrialization and specialization have dramatically increased food production levels over several decades. The only way that we can meet the challenge of feeding a population of over 7 billion people and growing is to continue to innovate, to use science and technology to help make production, processing and distribution even more efficient. Proponents of this argument will often add the corollary that the more efficient we make food production—the more that we can produce per unit of land—the more space and resources we can leave to other species. So there are ecological and biodiversity benefits to maximizing agricultural efficiency and intensity.

RESPONSES TO THE ARGUMENT FROM FEEDING THE WORLD

Several critiques of the *argument from feeding the world* have been developed. In what follows, I discuss the most influential of them.

IS INDUSTRIAL AGRICULTURE REALLY HIGHER YIELDING?

Claims about the productivity of organic vs. industrial agriculture and of monoculture vs. polyculture are highly contested. Industrial agriculture (also often referred to as *conventional agriculture*) refers to commodity monoculture that uses chemical fertilizers, herbicides and pesticides. It is also associated with the use of genetically modified crops (*GM crops*) and corporate control, the latter being effected through such things as seed patents and consolidated farm ownership. Organic agriculture is characterized by a rejection of the use of GM crops and chemical inputs. It employs non-synthetic fertilizers (such as manure), crop diversity and rotation, and integrated pest management. It is also historically associated with smaller independent farms, lower ecological impacts, and local or regional distribution systems. However, it should be noted that growing consumer demand for organics in affluent nations has led to a dramatic increase in what might be called *industrial organic production*—otherwise conventional agriculture that does not use GM crops or chemical inputs.

Which approach to agriculture results in higher yields is largely an empirical question that good research and data should help resolve. However, in this debate the science itself is contested, and each position has research and cases that they cite in support of their view. Nevertheless, some recent surveys of the literature are beginning to converge on the following picture. There appears to be a yield gap (as much as 25%) between organic and conventional agriculture for commodity grains grown in highly industrialized nations—e.g. corn grown in the United States and Brazil. However, the gap is much smaller (only around 5%), even in industrialized nations, for many other crops (e.g. legumes). Moreover, in less industrialized nations, where most food insecurity exists, organic and traditional farming sometimes match or exceed industrial yields. (These are sometimes referred to as *uncertified organics*.) Furthermore, several studies have found that there is room for significantly increasing yields in both types of agriculture—e.g. by increased nitrogen availability in organic agriculture and by increased crop diversity and improved use of crop residues in conventional agriculture (Seufert et al., 2012; De Schutter, 2011; Pretty and Hine, 2001; Pretty et al., 2003). So while it appears that there are yield differences between organic and conventional agriculture, what those differences are varies based on crop type and eco-social contexts.

WHAT COUNTS AS HIGHER YIELD?

Several prominent critics of the global industrial food system—e.g. Michael Pollan, Frances Moore Lappé and Vandana Shiva—argue that even when there are "increases" in yield associated with industrial agriculture, they are only apparent increases. One reason for this is that calculations of industrial monoculture's greater production over traditional polyculture fail to account for all the types of food plants grown in polycultural practice. For example, Shiva reports that in smallholder Indian agriculture, women cultivate 150 different species of plants for food and other uses, including health care, that in Sub-Saharan Africa women cultivate up to 120 species, and that in Thailand women cultivate as many as 230 species. As a result, studies that focus only on primary crops like soy or corn may systematically underreport polyculture's production levels.

Another criticism is that claims about industrial agriculture's "higher" yields are misleading because they do not incorporate the full costs associated with them. Even if industrial agriculture can produce more calories in a defined area in a growing season, one must also consider the impacts outside the system—e.g. that high water usage means less water available elsewhere (or in the future), that fertilizer runoff or animal waste disposal could harm local drinking water supplies and reduce riparian or ocean productivity, or that large amounts of inputs into the system are required. Critics argue that once all the *external* agricultural costs and impacts are *internalized* into the yield calculation, industrial agriculture is less efficient than organic agriculture or polyculture.

A third concern is that these same external impacts and high-input needs make sustaining high production levels more difficult for industrial agriculture in the long run. It also results in fields not being used in the secondary growing season—e.g. for cover crops and feed hay. So even if the primary season yield is elevated for a short time, it is offset by productivity losses in the secondary growing season and in the future.

IS MAXIMIZING YIELDS THE REAL CHALLENGE?

Some people have argued that the organic vs. conventional yield issue is a bit of a red herring. For one thing, as discussed above, if the goal is to maximize productivity, then in some cases conventional is better while in others organic is better, and very often some hybrid approach incorporating elements of the two will be higher yielding. Moreover, because there is room for increasing yields with both approaches, it may be that each has the capacity to produce enough calories and nutrition to feed the world.

Furthermore, the challenge of feeding the world is as much about food *distribution, access* and *usage* as it is about production. There is *currently* enough food for everyone to have sufficient calories and nutrition (FAOSTAT, 2013; FAO, 2013c): "The average dietary energy supply adequacy, which expresses the dietary energy supply as a percentage of the average dietary energy requirement, has increased globally from 114 to 120 in the last 20 years. At the same time, the share of energy provided by cereals, roots and tubers has been gradually shrinking, reaching 51 percent in 2007–9. The amount of available protein per person per day increased by 13 percent at the world level between 1990–92 and 2007–9" (FAOSTAT, 2013, p. 76). The *dietary energy requirement* for a person differs based on age, sex and activity level. For each country, "the minimum energy requirement is the weighted average of the minimum energy requirements of the different gender-age groups" in the country and on the most recent estimates ranged from 1,690 kcal/person/day to 1,990 kcal/person/day (FAOSTAT, 2010; FAOSTAT, 2008a).

Average dietary energy supply adequacy exceeds 100 in *every developing region*—including Sub-Saharan Africa and Southern Asia, which have the highest rates of malnutrition—though not in every nation (FAOSTAT, 2013). In aggregate, the average dietary energy supply adequacy in developing regions increased from 108 to 118 between 1990–92 and 2001–13 (FAO, 2013c). The nutritional quality of diets in developing regions also improved: "For example, per capita availability of fruits and vegetables, livestock products and vegetable oils increased by 90, 70 and 32 percent, respectively, since 1990–92 … Only Africa and Southern Asia did not benefit fully from these improvements" (FAO, 2013c, p. 18).

Although there is enough food and nutrition for everyone, 2 billion people suffer the effects of micronutrient deficiency and 842 million people are chronically undernourished and severely food insecure. Nearly 200 million children under the age of five are underweight, and over 2.5 million children die from malnutrition each year (FAO, 2012b). In Sub-Saharan Africa and Southern Asia, 35% to 40% of children under five are stunted from chronic caloric and nutrient deficiency (UNICEF, 2011). In some countries, such as Egypt, Kazakhstan, Nicaragua and Malawi, there is widespread stunting of young children (20% to 45%) despite their having dietary supply adequacy well above average requirements (110% to 145%) (FAOSTAT, 2013).

The issue of food insecurity will be discussed at length in the next chapter. Here, the point is that improving distribution and access is as important as improving yields when it comes to feeding the world. One key to doing so is addressing global poverty. As incomes of the global poor rise, diets improve and diversify— particularly with respect to protein sources, fruits and vegetables— and stunting, undernourishment and underweight rates all decline (FAO, 2012b; FAO, 2013c; FAOSTAT, 2013). Often, the problem is not that there is no food around, but that many people cannot afford it or cannot gain access to it. It is possible to dramatically increase food availability without increasing crop yields.

Another prominently discussed strategy for increasing food availability is improving caloric and nutrient utilization, particularly by reducing meat production. Feeding grains to animals that we then eat is a highly inefficient utilization of agricultural resources, since they use calories and nutrition for all sorts of things besides growing tissue. Approximately 41% of crop calories are lost from the food system because they are passed through animals or used for non-food purposes, such as the production of biofuels. How much agricultural production is lost from the food system due to inefficient utilization patterns varies dramatically by country. In India, 90% of crop calories go to human consumption, while only 34% do so in the United States. If the United States dedicated all of its crop calories to direct human consumption, those calories could feed three times as many people as they currently do (Cassidy et al., 2013). Within the global food system, agricultural production is a commodity, and the resulting crops will become feed or fuel (as opposed to being directly consumed by people) if that is where the market pays best.

Yet another way to dramatically increase food availability is to reduce food loss. The FAO estimates that one third of the food produced for human consumption is lost to the food system globally (FAO, 2013a). The percentage of food loss is roughly the same in both developed and developing nations. However, the losses are differently distributed within the food system. In less developed countries, the losses are predominantly at the production, transport and processing stages through spoilage and pests. In contrast, in affluent nations—where there is robust infrastructure, food abundance and food abundance and low food expenditure relative to household incomes—the majority of food loss occurs in the form of wastage at the retail and consumption stages. Food wastage will be discussed in more detail in the next chapter. Again, the point for present purposes is that there are ways to dramatically increase global food availability and reduce malnutrition other than by increasing crop yields (Foley et al., 2011).

ARGUMENT FROM PREFERENCE SATISFACTION

The second central argument in support of the global food system is that no other system can deliver to consumers what they want, when they want it, at a price they are willing to pay. In economics, a market or system is considered well functioning or efficient to the extent that it satisfies people's preferences. The global food system is extremely efficient at satisfying people's culinary preferences.

Those of us who live in affluent nations can get exactly the food we want at almost any time of the year. This applies not only to processed foods (e.g. cereals, ice cream, flavored drinks, chips and spreads), but also to fresh foods (e.g. meat, cheeses, fruits and vegetables) and to dining out (e.g. Mexican, Indian, Chinese, Italian and Japanese). Only a global food system can deliver berries to New England and citrus to Northern Europe in the middle of winter and provide a constant supply of fresh-caught tuna and salmon to Chicago and London. In the United States, for example, 91% of seafood (NOAA, 2013) and 38% of fresh fruits and nuts are imported (USDA, 2012a). The UK imports £2.6 billion in seafood and produces only 23% of the fruits and vegetables it consumes (resulting in a £7.3 billion fruit and vegetable trade gap) (DEFRA, 2012).

Moreover, all these foods are available at prices people are willing to pay: $1 USD for a double cheeseburger; $15 USD for a lobster dinner; $2.99 USD/pound for sweet cherries. The global food system makes this possible by driving down costs in the ways discussed earlier: global sourcing, minimizing labor costs, specialization, vertical integration, standardization, and economies of scale. In the United States, average household food expenditures are now 10% of household income, whereas in 1950 they were over 20%. In the UK, average household expenditures on food are only

11.6% of total expenditures. That those of us in affluent nations with food abundance spend so small a proportion of our incomes on food means that we can be choosier. We can pay a bit more for what we want when we want it, since we do not need to make our choices on the basis of cost and nutritional content alone.

One thing people increasingly want, all over the world, is convenience: fast food, processed food, prepared food, restaurant food, and food delivered to their doors. In Europe and the United States, the number of meals that people eat out per week has been rising for years. Prepared, processed and packaged "value-added" foods—from frozen dinners to Doritos—have accounted for the majority of growth in the United States food economy since the 1950s (USDA, 2014a). In the UK, 81% of food imports are highly processed (37%) or lightly processed (44%) (DEFRA, 2012). People are not buying more bulk and fresh foods to cook in their homes. They are going out to eat more frequently and bringing home more foods that are ready-to-eat (or nearly so). Processed foods have also been increasingly adopted in developing nations in large part because they enable longer storage in the absence of reliable electricity/ refrigeration and can ease the very significant time and labor burdens associated with food preparation. Just as washing machines freed people (particularly women) from the burden of laundering by hand, processed foods can free people (particularly women) from the burden of preparing food from scratch.

The global food system is a market system that responds to consumer demands. No other system could reliably deliver the variety of foods that people want, when they want them, at the price they are willing and able to pay. That is, no other food system can satisfy people's food needs and preferences so well as a global industrial food system. Because an economic system works well to the extent that it satisfies people's preferences, and the global food system satisfies preferences so well, we ought to embrace the global food system, according to this argument.

RESPONSES TO THE ARGUMENT FROM PREFERENCE SATISFACTION

As with the argument from feeding the world, several critiques of the *argument from preference satisfaction* have been offered. In what follows, I discuss the most influential of them.

The argument from preference satisfaction is based on the normative premise that a system or policy is well justified to the extent that it satisfies people's preferences. This premise is underwritten by the value claim that satisfying preferences is good and frustrating preferences is bad, regardless of what the preferences are. However, many ethicists have argued that it is also important to evaluate the preferences themselves. Preferences can be uninformed or based on false information. For example, people might have preferences for a certain kind of meat dish based on its aesthetic qualities, but be uninformed about the way animals are treated during its production. This information, if it were available, might alter people's preferences. It may even be that in some cases additional information *should* alter people's preferences. That is, ethical considerations can make preferences unendorsable. For example, if we find that a product is produced by exploiting people or in ways that are ecologically destructive, and this is the only way it can be done at a marketable rate, the appropriate response is to give up the preference. Many people have argued that this applies to preferences for eating tropical foods in the North during the winter, as well as to inexpensive foods eaten from many fast food restaurants. Given the ecological costs and worker treatment involved, we ought not have such preferences. Some extend this critique to the global food system generally. The global food system might be the only way to give us what we want, when we want it, at a price we are willing to pay, but the system is so ethically problematic (for reasons discussed below), that we must give up those preferences rather than retain the system, according to this critique.

We can also have preferences that are inconsistent with our own ethical commitments or that are based on poor reasoning. For example, we might believe that everyone who works a full-time job deserves a living wage, but also want access to as inexpensive food as possible. These two preferences are in tension with each other, since a commitment to a living wage for everyone implies a willingness to pay a bit more for the things they produce. Therefore, rational consistency requires that we revise our preferences. Preferences also can be inauthentic. For example, they can be the product of external manipulation, rather than internal reflection. This concern often is raised regarding food advertising, particularly when it is targeted toward young children: the advertising can be misleading, manipulative, or play on our insecurities or cultural biases. (This issue is discussed in Chapter 5.) Another way in which preferences can be manipulated is by controlling the conditions of their formation. For example, people might have preferences for large amounts of meat in their meals only because the cost of meat is artificially low due to subsidies and cost externalization. Finally, our preferences can be bad for us. In the case of food, we very often have unhealthy preferences (even knowingly so). The fact that we want sugary drinks and buttery sauces does not mean it is good for us to have them. There are thus quite a lot of reasons to think that preference satisfaction is not always good.

WHOSE PREFERENCES ARE SATISFIED?

A second response often raised to the argument from preference satisfaction concerns not the content of our preferences, but their distribution. The concern is that the global food system excels at satisfying the food preferences of affluent people living in countries of food abundance—we are able to get any food we want, from anywhere in the world, at a price we are willing to pay—but the preferences and even basic needs of others go unmet. This is evidenced by the 842 million undernourished people in the world. What is more, this critique maintains, the industrial features of the global food system that make food less expensive in affluent countries actually diminish food security and come at a cost to people in less developed countries. There are several ways in which this is thought to occur.

One way is through the displacement of local and smallholder agriculture and fishing. This can occur through the detrimental ecological impacts of industrial production. For example, intensive high-impact shrimp aquaculture in Southern Asia has expanded rapidly in recent decades, resulting in reduced water quality, wetland loss and mangrove deforestation. This makes it more difficult for smaller-scale fishing activities, since it dramatically reduces the quality and number of other aquatic species. It also detrimentally impacts coastal agriculture by increasing water salinity. Another cause of displacement is direct competition. In many places where fishing has been a primary food source, industrial trawling has reduced fishing stocks, particularly in coastal waters, displacing local fishermen and increasing food insecurity. In Tanzania's Lake Victoria, for example, commercial fishing of Nile perch (an introduced species) has displaced local fishermen, disrupted social systems, and resulted in dramatic declines in food access and quality. Displacement also occurs with smallholder crop agriculture, through corporate land purchases, drawing down of the water table (combined with the capital costs of digging deeper wells), and pollution from synthetic chemical inputs.

A second way in which industrial agriculture is thought to be detrimental to the food security of the global poor concerns the dependencies created with a shift from polyculture for direct human consumption to commodity monoculture. With commodity agriculture, growers are dependent upon income from sales to purchase food diversity (or food at all, if the crops are non-food, such as ornamental flowers). However, global markets can be volatile in ways that undermine food security for smallholding farmers (who are often net food buyers) and poor consumers (who spend a large amount of their income on food and do not have income surplus). This occurred in 2006–8, when global food prices spiked and malnutrition rates of the very poor and smallholding farmers rose. (Higher prices can increase incomes for farmers who are net food sellers, but this is not a group with high levels of food insecurity.) Increases in malnutrition rates were much less dramatic in countries that had export controls, since higher global food prices did not pull as much food out of their economies and did not result in as large domestic price increases (FAO, 2011). In addition, once a country opens up to global food commodity trade, producers in that country can be undercut by lower-cost imports.

A third way in which the global food system is thought to promote poverty and food insecurity is through a global "race to the bottom." Global sourcing enables manufacture to occur wherever labor costs are lowest and regulations are weakest. The global competition to draw manufacturing therefore involves providing these conditions, which are ripe for worker exploitation and ecological degradation. This occurs with manufacture of many inexpensive consumer goods—from cell phones to plastic toys—and is prevalent in agro-food processing and manufacturing.

In response to these concerns, proponents of the global food system emphasize the capacity for agriculture and low-skill manufacturing to contribute to economic growth. Food insecurity is tightly tied to income level, and many countries have used low-wage, low-skill manufacturing as a stepping-stone for economic development. It may be true that there are initial costs and vulnerabilities, this argument acknowledges, but over time manufacturing infrastructure is developed and higher-skilled, higher-value manufacturing and employment emerge. This could occur as well with agro-food processing and manufacturing. Moreover, in resource-poor, low-income countries the very poor share in more of the benefits from agricultural growth than from non-agricultural growth, since people working in agriculture tend to live in rural areas and agricultural growth helps to reduce food prices (FAO, 2012b). However, the economic and malnutrition reduction benefits of agricultural growth that accrue to the very poor are much lower when landholding is unequal (i.e. when fewer of the very poor are themselves landholders). For example, it has been more impactful in China and Vietnam (where landholding is relatively equal) than in India (where it is less equal). On large farms that are highly mechanized and owned by foreign entities (individuals or corporations), agricultural growth is not accompanied by increased employment for the very poor, and fewer economic gains remain in local communities, resulting in much less poverty reduction. Thus, agricultural growth contributes most to poverty reduction in developing nations when small and medium-sized landholders increase production beyond subsistence and are able to participate in the market. When that occurs, more food is available to create downward pressure on prices, landholders realize economic gains, and both farm and non-farm employment is generated.

IS IT ALL ABOUT PREFERENCES?

A third concern regarding the preference satisfaction argument for the global food system is that it overstates the value or importance of satisfying people's preferences. One reason for this, discussed above, is that preference satisfaction is not always good in itself. However, a second reason is that there are many other significant values involved in the global food system besides need and preference satisfaction. These values form the basis for the concerns about the global food system discussed in the next section.

CONCERNS ABOUT THE GLOBAL FOOD SYSTEM

A number of concerns have been raised regarding the global food system. Almost all of them are related to its global and industrial features. They arise from the belief that aspects of the system or its impacts either undermine important values or violate ethical principles.

FOOD AUTONOMY AND FOOD SOVEREIGNTY

Food autonomy is the capacity of a region to produce enough food to meet the nutritional needs of its population. *Food sovereignty* is the ability of a region to make decisions regarding its own food and agricultural practices and policies. The global food system is thought to undermine food autonomy and food sovereignty in several ways already discussed above. Its global character and focus on commodity production creates market-based vulnerabilities. International free trade agreements restrict governments from acting to protect their own farmers and agriculture sectors. Patents on seeds prevent farmers from saving them for future use and sharing them with others. High-input costs make farming more capital intensive and create dependencies and debts that, if unpaid, can result in farmers losing their land, which can also occur if landholders are unable to secure credit, a particular challenge for women. Monoculture makes regions less micronutrient independent. Competition from corporately owned farming and fishing operations can displace small-scale farmers and fishers. Globalized supply chains can make it more difficult for smallholding farmers to get their produce to market or to get full value for it (due to chain complexity, capital costs, instability of production, or crop size, for example).

Thus, one of the primary concerns about the global food system is that it decreases local, regional and national autonomy and sovereignty. One way this concern is frequently expressed is in terms of *corporate control of the food supply*. The idea that this phrase is meant to express is that in a global industrial system, large actors have disproportionate influence on such things as technology access, supply chain organization, and national and international policies, and they use this influence in ways that benefit themselves and disempower communities and individuals.

COMMUNAL PRACTICE AND CULTURAL DIVERSITY

The impacts on food autonomy and food sovereignty discussed above have secondary effects on cultural practices and traditions around agriculture and food. For example, the Indian activist Vandana Shiva has been prominent in articulating the ways in which corporate patents on seeds undermine rituals and practices around seed saving and sharing, which are crucial to the social fabric of rural communities in India and elsewhere. Displacement of local landholders also disrupts communal structures and familial roles that stretch back for generations.

The increased prevalence of convenience and processed foods in both affluent and developing nations has reduced the amount of time that people, families in particular, spend preparing and consuming food together. This results in losses of cultural knowledge and skills in food preparation, and it changes familial interactions and relationships. The globalization of processed foods and fast foods has also resulted in shifts in eating habits. Concerns are frequently raised regarding homogenization, and so cultural loss, in diets as more and more people drink the same sodas, eat at the same fast food restaurants, and purchase the same processed groceries.

Industrialization favors standardization due to the efficiency and stability it provides. A reliable, timely, cost-effective supply chain and processing procedure is much easier to establish if all the tomatoes or chickens are the same variety and size regardless of where they are sourced, and if all the processing facilities have similar infrastructures and technologies. Thus, concerns about homogenization apply as much to the varieties of foods and animals that are produced and raised, and the methods by which they are transported and processed, as they do to the products that are ultimately brought to market.

WORKERS' RIGHTS AND WELL-BEING

The industrial and market imperative to decrease prices for consumers and increase profits results in a strong incentive to reduce labor costs—to pay agricultural and food industry workers as little as possible and to provide them with as few benefits as possible. Thus, one of the primary concerns about the global food system is the way in which it fosters exploitation and mistreatment of workers.

In the United States, for example, the majority of hired agricultural workers are immigrants who speak little or no English. Approximately half of hired farm workers are undocumented immigrants (NAWS, 2004). As a population, they are socially, politically and legally marginalized. They often have few rights (and little knowledge about the rights they do have). They are at risk of deportation or replacement. They are unfamiliar with political institutions (and do not speak the language in which these institutions are administered). They are transient or migrant. They are invisible to consumers (i.e. there is no information about them on the products they produce). These are conditions that make exploitation possible: disempowered people with little or no form of recourse available to them. The average wage of hired farm workers is between $8 USD and $9 USD/hour, which is below a living wage, and health insurance and benefits are rarely provided. Working conditions often do not meet legal standards with respect to such things as workplace safety, security, chemical exposure, workday length, breaks, sanitation, water availability, housing, and full and timely payment. The agriculture industry has the highest rate of fatal occupational injuries and one of the highest rates of nonfatal injuries in the United States (and this does not take into account longitudinal pollutant exposure and musculoskeletal injuries).

Food industry workers are in a similar situation. In the United States, there are 2.4 million restaurant food preparation and service workers. They earn an average hourly wage of just under $9 USD/hour and have a median age over 28 (Bureau of Labor Statistics, 2014). With respect to fast food workers in particular, the vast majority have high school degrees, 40% are 25 and older (only 30% are teenagers), 58% are women, and over 25% have children (Schmitt and Jones, 2013). The total annual earnings of a person working full time at an hourly rate of $9 USD is below the federal poverty line for a family of three ($19,090 USD). (The United States minimum wage, which 13% of fast food workers earn, is $7.25 USD/hour.) The fast food industry also has among the highest rates of workplace injuries, particularly for teenagers, the shortest turnover periods, and the fewest opportunities for advancement. Most workers receive little or no health benefits.

The global sourcing of inputs and processes that favors the "race to the bottom" often results in agro-food workers in less developed countries having even fewer protections and rights than do workers in the United States. They are exposed to pesticides and herbicides, receive low compensation, have little if any redress for workplace mistreatment, are easily replaced, and work in unsafe and unsanitary conditions. Not all agro-food workers are poorly treated, of course, but the concern is that the global food system incentivizes and provides opportunities for it.

ECOLOGICAL IMPACTS

The ecological impacts of the global food system are enormous. Over a third of the terrestrial surface of the Earth is used for agriculture. Approximately 13 million hectares of forest are cleared for agriculture each year. Globally, 70% of all freshwater usage is for agriculture (in the United States, it is 80%) (USDA, 2013b; Aquastat, 2014). Habitat destruction is currently the largest contributor to biodiversity loss, and agriculture is the primary cause of it. The agriculture and forestry sectors are responsible for 24% of greenhouse gas emissions, and are thereby two of the largest contributors to global climate change (IPCC, 2014). In the United States alone, nearly 900 million pounds of pesticides and herbicides, and more than 12 million tons of fertilizer (nitrogen, phosphate, potash/potassium), are used each year, which has detrimental impacts on air and water quality, and which can result in aquatic "dead zones" (hypoxic areas produced by agricultural runoff, generating high nutrient loads, or eutrophication, which results in excessive microorganism growth). Each year, 56 billion land animals are raised for human consumption, and they produce a tremendous amount of waste—e.g. a single cow produces approximately 100–140 pounds of it each day (FAOSTAT, 2008b; EPA, 2011). Livestock can also contribute to riparian erosion, soil compaction, and devegetation. 87% of the world's fisheries are fully exploited or overexploited, and intensive aquaculture often results in water quality degradation and habitat loss. Industrial fishing practices, such as long-lining and trawling, are destructive to aquatic systems and nontarget species.

It is not possible to produce food for over 7 billion people without using quite a lot of land and water, or without capturing large amounts of plants and animals. However, critics of the global food system argue that the ecological impacts need not be so great as they currently are. As discussed earlier, many proponents of organic agriculture believe that synthetic chemical inputs can be eliminated and enough food still produced. Many people also argue that global supply chains result in very high transportation-related emissions and pollution, which could be dramatically reduced through regional or local systems. The term *food miles* is used to draw attention to the distance that foods and their ingredients travel before we consume them. Others have focused on the impacts of animal agriculture, particularly *concentrated animal feed operations* (CAFOs), which involve raising large numbers of animals in confined spaces where feed is brought to them (rather than in open spaces where they range for it). In the United States, there are nearly half-a-million CAFOs, including dairies, cattle feed lots, hog farms and poultry farms. CAFOs are common and expanding in Western Europe (e.g. the Netherlands and the UK), as well as in parts of Central and South America and Asia. These farms generate enormous amounts of waste that, if not managed properly, can contaminate rivers and aquifers with pathogens, high nutrient loads, antibiotics, hormones and organic matter. Critics argue that moving animals out of CAFOs and back onto pastures and range lands in sustainable numbers and integrating them with crop agriculture—e.g. rotating them into fields to control weeds and pests, and using their waste for fertilizer—would allow for meat production without the detrimental ecological impacts. (CAFOs will be discussed at greater length in Chapter 3.)

The industrial and market-based features of the global food system favor externalizing costs—i.e. passing them on to others—in order to reduce prices and increase profits. At present, the economic, ecological and human health costs associated with greenhouse gas emissions, nitrogen eutrophication, and the other ecological impacts of the global industrial food system are not fully priced into the cost of production and consumption.

ANIMAL WELFARE

The industrial character of the global food system favors commodifying all elements of food production, processing and distribution.

This was discussed earlier with respect to agro-food workers. If the goal of the system is to reduce consumer prices and increase profits, and there is a global labor pool, then there is an incentive and opportunity to develop a standardized, replaceable and low-cost labor force. Approximately 56 billion land animals and 90 billion aquatic animals are used each year in food production (FAOSTAT, 2008b). The same industrial and economic incentives to lower costs and facilitate production apply to them. This has resulted in a number of standard practices, particularly in CAFOs, which raise concerns about animal treatment and welfare. Regarding poultry, objections are commonly raised to the use of small wire battery cages to house birds in egg production facilities and to the debeaking and declawing performed in high-density broiler pro-duction. ("Broilers" is the term used to refer to chickens intended for human consumption. It categorizes them as food-for-people and illustrates the way in which language is often used not only to reference but to claim. Other examples of this include referring to wild animals as "game," aquatic systems as "fisheries," and forests as "timber.") Regarding hogs, there are objections to breeding sows in gestation crates, in which they cannot stand or turn around, as well as to tail docking and castration of males to increase docility and improve taste. Regarding cattle, there are concerns about branding, breeding techniques, use of growth hormones and antibiotics, improper diet, and the slaughtering process.

Whether these are practices that we should be concerned about depends upon whether we ought to care about the welfare of ani-mals. This is a topic discussed at length in Chapter 3. Here, the point is that industrialized production designed to meet the global demand for low-cost meat results in practices intended to increase the efficiency and lower the cost of production. Many of these practices involve treating animals in ways that cause them to suffer, and many people find this objectionable.

DISTRIBUTIVE JUSTICE

Among the core values embedded in the global industrial food system are maximizing the efficiency of production and economic outcomes. A concern often raised regarding systems or policies that aim at this sort of maximization is that they are inattentive to issues related to distribution. *Distributive justice* concerns the allocation of benefits and burdens. A system, policy or practice is thought to be unjust if those who benefit from it do not also shoulder the associated burdens, or if the benefits of the system are unequally distributed without good reason. For example, *environmental injustice* refers to the elevated rates of environmental hazards—e.g. factories, power plants, waste-treatment facilities and transportation depots—faced by high-minority and low-income communities. *Climate injustice* refers to the fact that climate change disproportionately impacts the global poor because they are more ecologically vulnerable and have the fewest resources with which to adapt to changing eco-social conditions, even though they are the least responsible for causing the problem, since they have comparatively small consumption levels and carbon footprints. *Economic injustice* refers to situations where economic growth increases incomes for the wealthy while the economic situation of the poor and middle class worsens.

Food justice concerns the allocation of benefits and burdens within the food system. Several food justice issues have already been discussed. For example, that agro-food workers often are poorly compensated and exposed to mistreatment that others benefit from in the form of lower prices and greater profits is considered by many to be unjust. That international and national trade, agriculture and fishery policies often favor corporations and large capital-rich landholders (or fleetholders) while being detrimental to independent producers and smallholders (or fishers) is also considered by many to be unjust. Furthermore, inequalities in food availability are often considered to be forms of injustice. For example, *food deserts* refer to areas in affluent nations, typically high-minority and low-income communities, where affordable high-quality nutritional foods (e.g. fruits and vegetables) are not readily available. *Global food justice* refers to the fact (already discussed) that enough calories are produced to feed everyone in the world, and yet 842 million people remain chronically undernourished, while others have so much food that a third of it goes to waste. *Environmental justice* is also an issue with respect to food systems, since agriculture has such large ecological impacts and there is an incentive to externalize the ecological and health costs of production. For example, intensive aquaculture and CAFOs often result in hazards, such as poor water and air quality, that are borne by local communities.

Food justice issues are frequently compounded by the ways in which they intersect with historical injustices. For example, in the United States, issues of environmental justice and food deserts are often understood through a civil rights and racism framework. (For this reason, environmental injustice is sometimes also referred to as *environmental racism*.) In some less economically developed nations, as well as among many indigenous peoples, issues of food security, food autonomy and food sovereignty are often understood as being continuous with historical injustices associated with military and economic colonialism.

Overall, the concept of food justice encapsulates a variety of issues associated with how and to whom the burdens and benefits of the global food system are distributed. As with other concerns about the system, these issues are not taken to be accidental side effects. Instead, they are thought to arise from fundamental features of the system—i.e. the drive to lower prices, the power of large actors, and the imperative to maximize efficiency and externalize costs wherever and whenever possible.

CONSUMER HEALTH

The industrialization of agriculture and the rise of processed foods have generated a variety of consumer health concerns. One such concern is the exposure to chemical substances. Industrial crop agriculture uses large quantities of synthetic herbicides and pesticides, and concerns have been raised about their entering into the food supply through uptake by plants and residues on produce. Industrial animal agriculture typically uses antibiotics to prevent the spread of diseases in CAFOs and often uses growth hormones to increase the rate of growth and milk production. There are worries about the effects of these substances on consumers, particularly those who eat a high meat and dairy diet. There are also worries about the cumulative effect of the large number of food additives—colorings, preservatives, flavorings and fillers—that are used in processed foods.

Another consumer health concern is nutrition. It is sometimes argued that industrially produced fruits and vegetables contain fewer vitamins and nutrients than those grown organically, although recent studies have raised doubts about this claim, and that highly processed grains and animal products do not contain the complete range of proteins or amino acids that people need. The largest nutritional concern, however, is that processed foods and beverages tend to be high in calories and low in nutrition. They often contain sweeteners, such as high-fructose corn syrup, and have high fat content. For example, a McDonald's Double Quarter Pounder with Cheese contains 750 calories, 380 of which are from fat, and a 20-ounce Coca-Cola contains 275 calories and 75 grams of sugar. Industrial efficiencies, cost externalization and subsidies have made processed high-caloric foods often less expensive (particularly on a per-calorie basis) than fresh foods. In high-income countries, a diet high in fruits, vegetables, fish and nuts costs on average $1.50 USD more per day (approximately $550 USD more per year) than does a less healthy diet rich in processed foods, meats and refined grains (Rao et al., 2013). The expansion of inexpensive high-caloric processed foods has contributed to enormous increases in obesity rates worldwide. There are now nearly 1.5 billion overweight adults in the world, 500 million of whom are clinically obese. There are 170 million children under 18 who are overweight or obese, and three quarters of the 40 million children under the age of five who are overweight live in developing countries. In the United States, 35% of adults are obese (66% are overweight), and in the UK 26% of adults are obese. Overweight and obesity are associated with increased risk for many health problems, including heart disease, diabetes, stroke, cancer and osteoarthritis.

A third consumer health concern has to do with food safety. Industrialized, centralized production in which efficiency is maximized is thought to promote conditions that lead to food contamination throughout the production and supply chain—e.g. unsanitary field conditions, high animal densities, the use of marginally healthy animals, and inadequately trained food preparers. Food poisoning (or foodborne illness) has a wide range of causes, including viruses, bacteria, parasites, toxins and prions. Some of the more common pathogens in affluent nations are e. coli, salmonella, norovirus, listeria and campylobacter. The Centers for Disease Control and Prevention estimates that in the United States 48 million people (or 1 in 6) get sick, 128,000 people are hospitalized, and 3,000 people die each year from foodborne illnesses. In the UK, around 1 million people get sick, approximately 20,000 people are hospitalized, and 500 people die each year from foodborne illnesses (FSA, 2011).

The problem of food contamination and illness is even more acute in less industrialized countries. It is estimated that there are up to 2 billion cases of illness from food and water each year and that approximately 1.6 million people, most of whom are children under the age of five, die from diarrheal diseases (WHO, 2014). A major cause of this is that 2.5 billion people (36% of the world's population) lack adequate sanitation and that 768 million people lack reliable access to safe drinking water (WHO, 2014; UNICEF, 2013a). (Food safety and food health are discussed at greater length in Chapter 5.)

HIDDEN PROCESSES

Several thinkers—most notably the philosopher Albert Borgmann— have observed that industrialization separates the consumption of goods and services from the process of their production. If we want or need something, whether it is heat or shoes, we simply buy it. We do not need to know anything at all about how things are made, where they come from, who produced them, or where they go after we are done with them. Nor do we need to know how things work. If we have a problem with our computer or our heating system, we can simply purchase a service (a technician or a plumber) to fix them. All we have to do is spend some money and then hit the power button in order to get the Internet, or turn up the thermostat to get heat.

The hiddenness of production pervades food consumption. In the global industrial food system, processed and prepared foods are ubiquitous. All we need to do is choose what we want, pay for it, and eat it. We are not confronted with how the crop was grown, the conditions under which the animals lived, how the agro-food workers were treated, the process of manufacture, or what happens to the waste. (The exception is when there is voluntary labeling—e.g. "humanely produced," "fair trade" or "organic"—but that applies to a small portion of the food supply.) Food is from the grocery store or the restaurant. Even when we choose to cook for ourselves, we purchase already butchered meat wrapped in cellophane or produce labeled only with its country of origin.

The concern is that such hiddenness fosters thoughtlessness. Because the food production process is invisible to us, we are uninformed about it and are not required to confront it. We can set aside or avoid qualms we might have about animal suffering or worker exploitation because they are concealed, and just enjoy what is revealed: the food and its price point. As a result, we do not take appropriate responsibility for our food choices. We see them as merely choices of taste and price (and maybe health) when there is in fact much more involved. The strong separation of consumption from production in the global food system thereby encourages us to engage in ethical negligence, and it is thought to enable many of the problems discussed above.

AESTHETICS

A final concern about the global industrial food system is that it has made the product itself, the food, less interesting and poorer tasting. This concern connects with a number of issues discussed above: homogenization and standardization of the food supply, which results in a loss of diversity; intensive processing of foods and the extensive use of fillers, preservatives and additives; and the degradation of culinary traditions, knowledge and cultural practices (i.e. foodways).

Moreover, the characteristics that make something well suited to industrial production and the global supply chain—e.g. that it is lower cost, easily standardized, grows quickly, and can travel long distances—are often contrary to good flavor. The quintessential example of this is the tomato. For a global industrial supply chain, tomatoes need to be picked before they are ripe; they need to be tough; and they need to be a reliable size, shape and color. However, truly flavorful tomatoes are picked ripe off the vine; they are juicy and easily damaged; and they are variable in size, shape and color. The flavor, texture and appearance of fresh and locally produced foods are not compatible with the characteristics needed for inclusion in the global industrial food system.

Another concern is that appreciation of good food is being lost. Recognition of the beauty of food—its taste, texture and aroma—requires attentiveness, subtlety, refinement and experience. The worry is that fast foods and processed foods do not allow for the development of these. One reason is that the food itself lacks aesthetic quality. Other reasons are our attitudes toward food, as well as the contexts in which we consume it. When we see food primarily in terms of nutrition, cost, convenience or abundance, and when we eat it quickly, on the go, alone, or while we are doing other things, we choose foods with less aesthetic interest and are not focused on what qualities it does have. People are increasingly concerned that the aesthetics of food is lost on us and that the benefits of participating in a culture that appreciates food are lost to us.

THE ALTERNATIVE FOOD MOVEMENT

The *alternative food movement* refers to people and groups committed to promoting alternatives to the global industrial food system. Like the global food system, the alternative food movement is not centrally organized and is highly dynamic. It is constituted by individuals, families, food cooperatives, farmers, community organizations, student groups, restaurant owners, chefs, non-governmental organizations (NGOs), activists and others trying to eat independently of the global food system, develop alternative agro-food networks, and address the problematic features of the global food system. Here, I discuss several different aspects of the alternative food movement. These are not meant to characterize distinct organizations or ideologies, but rather a cluster of overlapping commitments and goals that are adopted by many who identify with the movement.

ORGANIC FOODS

Organic foods are distinguished by the processes by which they are produced. Organic agriculture does not use GM crops, synthetic chemical inputs, or antibiotics/hormones. Organic growers use techniques such as integrated pest management, crop diversity and rotation, cover crops, and manure fertilizing in order to control pests and weeds, enrich soil, and manage waste. There are many different regulatory definitions of "organic." According to the United States Department of Agriculture (USDA), "organic is a labeling term that indicates that the food or other agricultural product has been produced through approved methods. These methods integrate cultural, biological, and mechanical practices that foster cycling of resources, promote ecological balance, and conserve biodiversity. Synthetic fertilizers, sewage sludge, irradiation, and genetic engineering may not be used."

Justifications offered for organic food production and consumption include that it is more sustainable and has much lower ecological and biodiversity impacts than industrial agriculture, since it does not use synthetic chemicals. It is also taken to be better for consumers, since the varieties grown are thought to be more nutritious, better tasting, and free of chemical contaminants.

Although "organic" is often officially defined by production method, those in the *organic movement*, which has been expanding globally since the 1960s, frequently embrace a much broader set of commitments. They typically reject not only chemical monoculture, but also corporate industrialization more generally in favor of smaller independent farmers, local production, shorter food networks, whole (natural or less processed) foods, humane animal agriculture, and strong (or deep) ecological sustainability. However, as the demand for organic foods has grown, large agro-food corporations have increasingly brought foods to market that qualify as organic—i.e. foods that do not contain genetically modified organisms and that are not grown with synthetic inputs. The global food system excels at delivering to affluent consumers what they want, when they want it, at a price they are willing to pay, and people want affordable organics. As a result, the terms *local foods* and *slow foods* have emerged to capture some of the broader commitments formerly encompassed by *organic foods*.

LOCAL FOOD

The *local food movement* emphasizes the distance between where food is produced and where it is consumed. One aspect of this distance is spatial—that is, how far food travels before it is eaten. This is often referred to in terms of *food miles*, and it is a common claim that the average American meal travels 1,500 miles from farm to plate. This number is based on studies of fruits and vegetables that found that they were on average consumed around 1,500 miles from where they were produced. This is a small sample size, though, and when it comes to calculating the food miles for a product comprising many ingredients that are processed and assembled in multiple locations—e.g. a cheeseburger—the calculation is much more complex. For example, one study of strawberry yogurt (produced and consumed in Iowa) found that ingredients would travel an average distance of approximately 277 miles and that the total source distance of the yogurt would be approximately 2,216 miles (Pirog and Benjamin, 2005).

Another dimension of the distance between food production and food consumption that concerns *locavores*, those who identify with the local food movement, is social. Social distance refers to the large number of actors that comprise global supply chains, as well as their generally impersonal nature. Social distance is related to the hiddenness generated by industrialization. In a global industrial food system, we do not know—and often cannot even find out—where the ingredients in our food come from or who the farmers and workers are that grow and prepare it. The "social" interactions that consumers engage in are with the people who stock the aisles and work the registers. We do not have real relationships with those who produce our food; they are invisible to us. A related locavore concern is that people are so distant from the process of food production that they do not understand it. When food simply appears, on the shelf or set before us, abstracted from the process of its production, we do not need to think about the people or ecological systems that create it. This ignorance fosters dependence, lack of appreciation, and misinformed practices and policies.

Arguments for local foods appeal to the benefits thought to be associated with reducing the social and physical distance between producers and consumers by shortening the supply chain. These include: developing meaningful and caring relationships, appreciation and friendship between producers and consumers; building a sense of community; fostering an understanding of our connections to and reliance upon ecological systems; reducing the ecological impacts associated with food production and transport; creating informed consumers who take responsibility for their food choices; supporting local small farmers who are invested in their communities and stewards of the land; keeping the resources spent on food in the local economy (instead of distributed to shareholders); and improving the nutrition and taste of the food we eat.

The rapid growth in the local food movement in recent years is evidenced by the tremendous expansion in farmers' markets and community-supported agriculture (CSA), in which small, local farmers sell directly to consumers. For example, in the United

States, there has been a 464% increase in the number of farmers' markets since 1994, from 1,755 to 8,144 (USDA, 2013c).

SLOW FOOD

Whereas local food is in contrast to global food, *slow food* is in contrast to fast food. Slow Food as an organization emerged from demonstrations opposing the opening of a McDonald's franchise in Rome in the 1980s. Since then, it has expanded to include over 1,500 local chapters ("convivia") in over 150 countries. Slow Food's manifesto ties concerns about the industrialization of the food system to broader cultural critiques of "fast life." By slowing down food, committing to well-prepared aesthetically pleasing foods that are socially just and ecologically sustainable, the movement aims to challenge the industrial character of contemporary society, such as its frenetic pace, its focus on product over process, its emphasis on quantity over quality, its prioritization of the individual, and its homogeneity. On this view, we have lost track of the things that really matter for living well: relationships, aesthetics, experiences, diversity, and caring for others (human and nonhuman). Food is an ideal place to make a stand against fast culture, since it is central to daily life and cultural practice, and the effects of industrialization on it are so pernicious.

In recent years, Slow Food has increasingly connected its cultural critique and commitment to "good food" to many of the other concerns that motivate the alternative food movement: food sovereignty, food security, sustainability, animal welfare, worker rights, human dignity, and social justice.

FOOD JUSTICE

The *food justice movement* refers to organizations, activists and efforts to reduce injustice in the global food system and to use food as a means for addressing unjust inequalities more generally. The food justice movement is diverse with respect to the issues it addresses, the types of organizations involved, and how it pursues its goals. For example, *fair trade* organizations are concerned with eliminating exploitation in global trade practices by ensuring that farmers in developing nations receive a fair price for their goods and are empowered to protect the integrity of their communities and the agricultural and ecological systems that support them. They promote these ends by certifying transactions between companies and producers that meet standards of fairness and sustainability. Worker organizations—such as United Farm Workers of America and UNITE HERE—organize unions and protests aimed at improving the working conditions and compensation of agricultural and food industry workers. Community organizations promote accessibility to nutritional and good tasting foods, and the elimination of food deserts. Urban gardening organizations promote community gardens and orchards as sources of communal improvement, empowerment and independence, as well as places where culturally significant foods and practices can be incorporated into urban contexts. Large NGOs, such as Oxfam and Feed the Children, aim to raise awareness of global malnutrition and address the poverty that causes it by means of aid and intervention programs.

Whereas the history of Slow Food begins with a concern about food and expands from there to concerns about justice, food justice movements often begin with concerns about exploitation, mistreatment, inequality, disempowerment and social marginalization, and move from there to a concern about food. Advocacy for nutritious, culturally appropriate food access is understood as part of the fight for cultural and civil rights, community recognition and uplift, dignity and sovereignty, and environmental health and justice. Food is prominent in these efforts due to its centrality to communal life, cultural practice, public health, and self-determination.

CONCERNS ABOUT THE ALTERNATIVE FOOD MOVEMENT

The alternative food movement is largely motivated by what its proponents regard as deeply problematic features of the global industrial food system. However, the alternative food movement has itself been subject to a number of criticisms.

THE LIMITS OF LOCAL

One of the primary arguments against the local food movement is that local food production simply cannot provide enough food to population-dense areas. For most major urban areas—and most people in the world now live in cities—there is not sufficient cultivatable land, fish stocks or water resources within 50, 100 or 200 miles to feed 5, 10 or 20 million people, particularly without industrial intensification.

Critics often emphasize that the problem is even more acute when one considers not only calories, but also nutrition and diversity. In many areas in North America and Europe, exclusively local would mean going without coffee, tea, cane sugar, rice and other staple foods. It would everywhere mean eating seasonally, resulting in much more restricted diets during the non-harvest seasons. It would mean that migrants would not have access to culturally significant foods that could not be grown in the area. It would mean no imported "fine" or "gourmet" foods. It would mean no seafood away from the coast. Local means, overall, a much less interesting, much less secure, much less diverse, and much less abundant diet.

In response to these concerns, proponents of local foods acknowledge that there will be a drop in diet diversity. We will not be able to eat whatever we want whenever we want it—no tropical fruits in the global North in December. However, this is not a significant sacrifice. In fact, people who are committed to the values that localism embodies will enjoy and be pleased about eating in season squashes rather than pineapples and bananas. Many locavores also allow that some staple and specialty foods will need to come from further away; that "local" should encompass 250 or 500 miles (and so really be regional); that if there is a yield-affecting crisis (e.g. drought or natural disaster) it will be necessary to import from outside the region; and that there are situations in which localism is just not feasible.

Critics point out that these sorts of caveats represent slippage from the locavore ideal. They take it to show that local food systems cannot deliver everything we need from a food system— variety, affordability, abundance and reliability. There may be many benefits associated with supporting local agriculture and urban farming; and it may be good to do so. Nevertheless, on this view, local food systems by themselves are not robust enough to represent a true alternative to multi-regional or global systems.

A second argument against the local food movement is that the distance that food travels is actually a poor proxy for many of the things that those in the movement care most about. As discussed above, one of the primary concerns about the high number of food miles generated by the global food system is the energy consumed and the greenhouse gas emissions from transportation. This justification for eating local depends upon the carbon footprint of food tracking food miles—i.e. the more local the food, the smaller the carbon footprint (carbon dioxide is the most prevalent and significant greenhouse gas). However, how far food travels is only one factor associated with its energy and emissions profile, and often not the most important one. How the food is grown also matters. For example, local tomatoes grown in an energy-intensive greenhouse can have a higher carbon footprint than tomatoes grown in the sun and shipped from thousands of miles away. How the food is transported also matters. Food that travels in large quantities by train can have a smaller per-unit carbon footprint than smaller quantities of the same food that travel by truck over a shorter distance. How far consumers travel to purchase the food matters. Driving to many different stores to purchase local foods, rather than taking one short trip to a single store to buy everything, can significantly increase the carbon footprint of a meal. In United States households, only 11% of the emissions associated with food are from the transportation phases of its life cycle, whereas 83% are associated with the production phases (Weber and Matthews, 2008).

The point that critics of localism typically aim to make is not that consuming locally produced foods is wrong. There often are personal, social and ecological benefits associated with growing and eating locally. However, they argue, we must also recognize that there are significant limits to what local systems can provide and that "local" is not always a good indicator of things like animal welfare, ecological impact or product quality. For this reason, it is necessary to avoid making single-parameter evaluations about food—i.e. determining its goodness or badness on the basis of food miles alone. It is crucial to keep focused on what matters, and the distance that food travels is rarely its most ethically salient feature.

THE LIMITS OF ORGANIC

The primary argument against the organic movement is that without synthetic inputs, growth hormones, engineered crops and other technological innovations it will not be possible to produce enough food to feed a growing population of over 7 billion people. As discussed earlier in this chapter, there does appear to be a yield gap between industrial and organic agriculture for some crops grown under some conditions. However, research also suggests that organic methods may nevertheless be able to produce enough food for a nutritionally adequate diet for everyone, particularly in combination with changes in utilization patterns and reductions in food wastage. (This is discussed at greater length in the next chapter.)

A second argument against the organic movement is that organically produced foods tend to be more expensive than their conventionally grown counterparts. There are many reasons for this. One is that, because the certified organic supply is so small, there is a lower supply to demand ratio in many places. In the United Sates, for example, only 0.7% of total cropland is certified organic, according to the USDA. Even for the primary organic sectors, vegetables (6% organic) and fruits and nuts (4% organic), the vast majority of acreage is conventional. Another reason that organics are more expensive is that agricultural policies often aim to maximize yields and promote industrial commodity monoculture. A third reason is the costs associated with the organic certification process and ensuring that there is no "contamination" from conventionally grown crops. There are also features of organic production that make it more costly—e.g. greater labor demands, better treatment of animals, and less externalization of ecological costs. Moreover, insofar as organics are associated with independent, smaller farmers and processors (which, as discussed above, is not necessarily the case), there will not be the same efficiencies of scale and vertical integration as are found in industrial agro-food systems. An organic food system is not going to produce a one-dollar double cheeseburger. Because organic foods are more expensive, the organic movement is often charged with being elitist. Moreover, for those who are poor or food insecure, higher food prices would exacerbate their situation.

Finally, critics of the organic movement often argue that many of the benefits claimed for organic foods are spurious. For example, several studies have found that organic produce is neither significantly more nutritious nor significantly safer to consumers than their conventionally grown counterparts (Smith-Spangler et al.,

2012). Others point out that highly capitalized and science-intensive agricultural practices have in fact been decreasing the ecological impacts of conventional agriculture in recent years (OECD, 2013b). Still others emphasize that "organic" is now a less good proxy for small and independently owned agricultural operations than it has been in the past.

THE LIMITS OF SLOW FOOD

As discussed above, the slow food movement's origins were in opposition to fast food and fast society, and it emphasized food quality, aesthetic appreciation and communal consumption. However, the principles that it embraces have expanded to encompass a broad range of alternative food movement values and goals— food security, social justice, human rights, animal welfare, ecological sustainability, and cultural sensitivity. Critics of the movement argue that there are significant tensions within its value commitments and that these are manifest in how the slow food movement often works in practice.

One common criticism of the slow food movement is that it is elitist. Its emphasis on aesthetic quality and traditional production methods often lead it to valorize gourmet and artisanal foods, which tend to be expensive and not widely available. Critics also point out that the cost to join slow food groups and attend slow food events are often quite high, since the foods involved are expensive and the people who are drawn to the movement (and can afford to be a part of it) have "expectations" regarding such things as service and location. Moreover, slowness in food preparation and consumption presumes the availability of time, which many working families do not have. What is more, the movement denigrates the convenient and inexpensive processed and fast foods on which many poor and middle-class people depend.

Critics also point out that the slow food movement's prioritization of food aesthetics frequently undermines other values it espouses. For example, gourmet and artisanal foods are often shipped over long distances and have high food miles. Many slow food advocates also seem willing to compromise on the commitment to animal welfare when it comes into tension with traditional and delicacy food production, such as the production of veal and foie gras. Moreover, the movement's commitment to artisanal and gourmet foods, as well as "good food" more generally, has led some commentators to charge it with merely replacing one form of consumerism—convenient and inexpensive "fast" consumerism— with another—exclusive and luxury "slow" consumerism. Rather than rejecting consumeristic ideals, it has simply substituted an elitist, self-indulgent version for a populist one.

Another concern about the slow food movement is that its founding commitment—a rejection of industrially produced processed foods—is problematic. While acknowledging that there are many problems with the industrial food system as it is now, many commentators argue that we must also recognize the benefits that food technology and industrialization provide. One, already discussed, is that it has increased yields and the efficient use of resources. Another is that prepared and processed foods can be transported and stored more easily and for longer periods of time than fresh foods, which increases food safety and reduces spoilage. It also increases the diversity and amount of food available during non-harvest seasons, thereby promoting food security. Prepared and processed foods also enormously reduce the burden of food production and preparation. This frees up those responsible for food preparation—predominantly women—for other activities, including going to school and participating in the workforce and civic life. Convenience foods really are convenient, and for many people this is of tremendous value in their already very busy and demanding lives.

Other critics of the slow food movement charge it with false nostalgia. Proponents of slow food seem to imagine that prior to food industrialization the world was full of people eating good-tasting, locally sourced and abundant foods. However, food historians have pointed out that for most people, the situation prior to industrialization was one of limited diets, marginal foods, and an annual challenge to get through the "hunger season" between when the previous year's harvest (or catch) runs out and when new crops and food sources become available.

The overarching argument against the slow food movement is that it is misguided. Its rejection of fast and processed foods is blind to the tremendous benefits that those foods and the system that enables them provide. Moreover, it fails to see how its commitments to slowness and "good food" are just another (more elitist) form of consumerism, which undermines social justice, ecological sustainability, and other values that it professes to embrace. Finally, proponents of slow food appear to believe that the primary food challenge we face is one of people with food abundance making poor food choices, when the real problem is that there are 842 million people in the world who do not have enough to eat.

THREE QUESTIONS ABOUT FOOD SYSTEMS

Here are three key questions to consider about the food system debate, which also bear on the topics discussed in the chapters that follow.

1. ARE THE PROBLEMATIC FEATURES ASSOCIATED WITH THE GLOBAL FOOD SYSTEM INSEPARABLE FROM IT? OR CAN THE SYSTEM BE "CLEANED UP"?

As we have seen, many critiques of the global food system argue that the problems associated with it are due to its industrial and global character, and so are inherent in it. However, others have suggested that improved policies and practices could reduce or eliminate most of the problems. On this view, if there were living wage laws, enforcement of worker protections, compassionate animal handling standards, internalization of ecological costs, fair trade, and better consumer information, for example, we could have the advantages of a global food system—reliable access to low-cost, convenient and diverse foods—without the problems that the system currently has. In support of this position, proponents highlight that there already are successes in this respect—for example, food workers are paid a living wage in many countries, and many retailers (e.g. McDonald's) are requiring that their suppliers eliminate the use of gestation crates. In response, critics argue that even if this is possible in principle, the political realities and entrenched interests and power structures make it practically impossible. The more promising and preferable option is to build an alternative model. Moreover, they point out that if all the changes to the global industrial food system needed to "clean it up" were actually made, the result would be something very much like the system advocated by the alternative food movement.

2. DO AFFLUENT CONSUMERS HAVE A RESPONSIBILITY TO CHANGE WHAT THEY WANT AND EXPECT FROM THEIR FOOD SYSTEM?

People in affluent nations expect a wide variety of foods to be available, virtually all the time and at a reasonable cost. If a global industrial food system is needed in order to meet these expectations, and that system is socially, ecologically and ethically problematic, then do they have a responsibility to change their consumer preferences and behaviors? If so, which expectations or practices should they alter—their desire for out-of-season foods, for high-meat diets? Or is it possible to move to a more regional or local system without having to alter their expectations and behaviors in any significant respects?

3. IS A HYBRID SYSTEM DESIRABLE AND, IF SO, WHAT WOULD IT BE LIKE?

Global and alternative food systems are often presented as diametrically opposed. However, we have seen that the dichotomies associated with them do not always hold. Local foods do not always have a smaller ecological footprint. Organic foods do not always come from small, independently owned and operated farms. Global sourcing is frequently necessary for people to access culturally appropriate foods. Industrial agriculture does not always have higher yields. Agro-food workers are not always exploited. Processed and fast foods are not necessarily less healthy. Slow foods are not always more compassionate. Local systems are not always more food secure. This suggests that an ethically optimal food system might incorporate elements of both the global food system and the system advocated by the alternative food movement. If this is to be the case, what would that hybrid system be like? In what respects would it be industrial and in what respects would it be alternative? And would it differ with respect to context (e.g. urban vs. rural, affluent nation vs. developing nation)?

CONCLUSION

A fundamental issue in contemporary food ethics and policy is what sort of food system we ought to support and promote. In this chapter, I have reviewed the primary arguments in defense of the global industrial food system, some responses to those arguments, and criticisms of the system. I have also discussed the considerations offered in favor of alternative food systems, as well as concerns that have been raised regarding the alternative food movement. I have emphasized the ways in which food systems connect to other aspects of food ethics, including animal welfare, ecological sustainability, social justice, public health, aesthetics, technology use and food security. These topics are examined in greater detail in the chapters that follow.

FURTHER READING

Sources for the empirical data used throughout this book are cited in the text. The full references for them are located in the bibliography. These sources include scholarly journals, government agencies, NGOs, and reputable news organizations. There is a wealth of information and perspectives to be found in these articles, reports, databanks and publications.

Some general resources on the social and ethical dimensions of food include:

Paul Thompson and David Kaplan, eds., *The Encyclopedia of Food and Agricultural Ethics* (Springer)

Gregory Pence, ed., *The Ethics of Food: A Reader for the Twenty-First Century* (Rowman and Littlefield)

David Kaplan, ed., *The Philosophy of Food* (University of California Press)

Fritz Allhoff and Dave Monroe, *Food and Philosophy* (Wiley-Blackwell)

Peter Singer and Jim Mason, *The Ethics of What We Eat* (Rodale Press)

Paul Thompson, *The Agrarian Vision: Sustainability and Environmental Ethics* (University Press of Kentucky)

Food, Culture & Society (Bloomsbury), a journal published by the Association for the Study of Food and Society

Agriculture and Human Values (Springer), a journal of the Agriculture, Food, and Human Values Society

Agricultural and Environmental Ethics (Springer), a journal that publishes articles on ethical issues confronting agriculture, food production and environmental concerns

Renewable Agriculture and Food Systems (Cambridge University Press), a journal that focuses on economically, environmentally and socially sustainable approaches to agriculture and food production

Food Policy (Elsevier), a journal that focuses on formulation, implementation and analysis of policies for the food sector in both developing and advanced economies

Regarding food systems, some prominent and influential popular books critical of the global food system and supportive of the alternative food movement include:

Michael Pollan, *The Omnivore's Dilemma: A Natural History of Four Meals* (Penguin)

Vandana Shiva, *Stolen Harvest: The Hijacking of the Global Food Supply* (South End Press)

Eric Schlosser, *Fast Food Nation: The Dark Side of the All-American Meal* (Mariner Books)

Carlo Petrini, *Slow Food: The Case for Taste* (Columbia University Press)

Frances Moore Lappé, *Diet for a Small Planet* (Ballantine Books)

Anna Lappé, *Diet for a Hot Planet: The Climate Crisis at the End of Your Fork and What You Can Do about It* (Bloomsbury)

Wendell Berry, *The Unsettling of America: Culture and Agriculture* (Sierra Club Books)

Wes Jackson, *New Roots for Agriculture* (University of Nebraska Press)

Works that defend aspects of the global food system and that are critical of elements of the alternative food movement include:

Pierre Desrochers and Hiroko Shimizu, *The Locavore's Dilemma: In Praise of the 10,000-Mile Diet* (Public Affairs)

James McWilliams, *Just Food: Where Locavores Get it Wrong and How We Can Truly Eat Responsibly* (Back Bay Books)

Rachel Laudan, "A Plea for Culinary Modernism: Why We Should Love New, Fast, Processed Food," in *Gastronomica: The Journal of Food and Culture* (University of California Press)

Robert Paarlberg, *Food Politics: What Everyone Needs to Know* (Oxford University Press)

Two excellent books on the issue of food justice in particular are:

Alison Hope Alkon and Julian Agyeman, eds., *Cultivating Food Justice: Race, Class, and Sustainability* (MIT Press)

Robert Gottlieb and Anupama Joshi, *Food Justice* (MIT Press)

FOOD SECURITY AND
THE ETHICS OF ASSISTANCE

The number of people in the world who are undernourished has declined in recent years. Among the causes of this are increases in the food supply and decreases in extreme poverty. In all regions of the world, the amount of calories produced per capita has gone up over the last several decades, while the number of people living below the global "poverty line" of $1.25 USD ppp (purchasing power parity)/day has declined. Nevertheless, the number of people who live in extreme poverty and cannot meet their basic food needs remains staggering: 1.2 billion people live in extreme poverty (one third of whom are children under 12), and 842 million people are chronically undernourished, which means that they cannot meet their minimum daily energy and nutritional requirements (UN, 2013b; Olinto et al., 2013). This represents 12% of the global population. The vast majority of undernourished people (827 million) are in developing regions, particularly Sub-Saharan Africa, Eastern Asia and Southern Asia. In Sub-Saharan Africa, a quarter of the population is undernourished (FAO, 2013c).

The impacts of caloric and nutrient malnourishment include stunting, wasting, chronic health problems, increased susceptibility to diseases, and death. For example, the World Health Organization (WHO) estimates that 250 million children suffer from vitamin A deficiency, which results in 250,000 children going blind annually, half of them dying within a year of losing their eyesight. In several countries in Africa and Southern Asia, the stunting rates for children under five exceed 30% (FAO, 2013c). Stunting has developmental impacts with long-term effects on educational achievement and economic productivity. Thus, pervasive malnourishment has immediate impacts on people's welfare and presents longitudinal societal challenges.

One of the most important issues in food ethics is determining what people in affluent nations ought to do, at both the national and individual levels, in response to this situation. That is to ask: What are our obligations and responsibilities to address global poverty and malnutrition? This question is the topic of this chapter. I begin by discussing the causes of food insecurity and possible approaches to addressing it, before turning to the arguments for and against an ethical obligation to provide assistance.

SOURCES OF FOOD INSECURITY

The global malnourishment problem is often equated with a global population problem—i.e. the problem is simply that there are more people than can be supported with finite planetary resources. However, this conflates the problem with two of the factors that contribute to it and that are relevant for addressing it: population and resource base. The problem is that there are 842 million chronically undernourished people in the world. The challenge is feeding everyone a nutritionally adequate and culturally appropriate diet in a sustainable way that leaves adequate resources for other species. There are *many* factors that contribute to the problem and that are relevant to meeting the challenge, several of which were discussed in the previous chapter.

POPULATION

The more people there are, the more food is needed to feed everyone a nutritionally adequate diet (all other things being equal). There are already 7.2 billion people on Earth. Assuming a future fertility rate of 2.24 children per woman (the UN's medium fertility rate scenario), there will be 9.6 billion people in 2050 and 10.9 billion people in 2100. On the UN's high fertility variant, the number of people in 2100 is projected to be 16.6 billion. On the low fertility rate variant, the population in 2100 is projected to be 6.8 billion (UN, 2013a).

RESOURCE BASE

There are ecological and planetary limits relevant to food production. There is a finite amount of cultivatable land, fresh water and solar radiation, for example. Already, over a third of the terrestrial surface of the Earth, the vast majority of agriculturally favorable land, is used for food production (25% of which is degraded due to such things as topsoil loss, microbial diminishment and nutrient depletion) (FAO, 2013b). We already use approximately 25% of the planet's net primary plant production. Over 87% of the world's fisheries are fully exploited, overexploited, or recovering (15% to 20% of the animal protein consumed globally is from aquatic animals). Many crucial freshwater sources for agriculture—such as North America's Ogallala Aquifer—are being depleted much faster than they can be replenished.

AGRICULTURAL PRODUCTIVITY

Because population has grown while the agricultural resource base has remained comparatively constant, the amount of resources available per capita for food production has decreased. However, as discussed in the previous chapter, the amount of calories, protein and fat produced and available per capita today is greater than it was in 1960. Per capita production and supply vary significantly by region—e.g. North America and Europe produce far more kcal/person/day and have a much higher average dietary energy supply adequacy than do Africa and Asia. Nevertheless, every region in the world has an average dietary energy supply above 100—i.e. enough calories to meet everyone's dietary energy requirements. Moreover, diets in developing nations have become more nutritious and diverse due to the increased availability of fruits, vegetables, oils and animal products. The increase in food supplies has been accomplished through improvements in agricultural practices, innovation and dissemination of agricultural technologies (within both industrial and organic agriculture), and agricultural and capture expansion.

INCOME INEQUALITY AND CONSUMPTION PATTERNS

If there are enough calories and nutrition in the food supply for everyone, then food production constraints and population cannot be the entire explanation for why there are 842 million malnourished people in the world. Another significant factor is global poverty and income inequality. As discussed above, 1.2 billion people live below the extremely low poverty line of $1.25 USD ppp/day. That is, they try to live on less than the equivalent of what $1.25 USD would purchase in the United States in 2005 (Olinto et al., 2013). In a great many places, that amount (or even double that amount) is not enough to afford a nutritionally adequate diet. In 2007, the wealthiest 20% of the world's population earned nearly 83% of total global income, while the poorest 20% earned only 1% and the poorest 60% only 7.3%. The top 1% of earners (61 million people) had the same total income as the bottom 56% (3.5 billion people) (Ortiz and Cummins, 2011). Global wealth inequality is just as extreme as global income inequality. In 2012, the wealthiest 0.7% of adults in the world (those with a net worth of over $1 million USD) held 41% of the world's wealth, while the top 8.4% (the 393 million adults with a net worth of over $100,000 USD) held 83% and the lowest 68.7% (the 3.2 billion adults with a net worth of less than $10,000 USD) held only 3% (O'Sullivan and Kersley, 2012). There is, not surprisingly, a strong correlation between income/wealth and consumption, including both grain and animal product consumption (Ortiz and Cummins, 2011). Per capita food consumption is over four times greater in high-income countries than in low-income countries, and per capita consumption of animal products is as much as twenty times greater in high-income countries than in low-income countries.

RESOURCE UTILIZATION

In many places, the majority of calories produced are not delivered to the food system. This is the case in regions with high levels of per capita beef production, such as the United States, Europe, Brazil and Argentina. Producing nutrition through animals is extremely inefficient, since the animals use feed and water for many metabolic purposes besides growing tissue—e.g. breathing, moving, and growing hair, teeth and feathers. For example, producing 500 calories of beef requires 4,902 liters of water, whereas producing 500 calories of poultry requires 1,515 liters, 500 calories of beans 421 liters, and 500 calories of potatoes 89 liters. Similarly, the water used to produce 10 grams of protein from corn is only 130 liters, whereas for eggs it is 244 liters and for beef it is 1,000 liters (World Watch Institute, 2004; FAO, 2006). Only approximately 10% to 12% of calories fed to animals are ultimately consumed by people (this is in aggregate, the rate is higher for dairy and eggs than it is for meat consumption), and over a third of the calories and half the protein of food crops are fed to animals. Even insect rearing is far more efficient than raising livestock—for example, crickets need only 1/12 the feed of cattle to produce the same amount of protein—and insects are estimated to already be part of the regular diets of 2 billion people (van Huis et al., 2013).

Another way in which calories fail to reach the food system is that they are diverted for use in biofuel production. Biofuel from corn in the United States and sugarcane in Brazil alone accounted for 4% of crop calorie production globally in 2010. In the United States, over 300 million people could be fed with the calories used to produce biofuel, and over 80% of corn grown is used for animal feed and ethanol production (Love, 2010; Cassidy et al., 2013; USDA, 2014b). Moreover, a large amount of calories and nutrition in the food system are lost through wastage. It is estimated that in the UK 15 million tons of food is thrown away each year and that in the United States as much as 40% of food that enters the food system is lost to waste. Even in less developed countries, losses to food waste and spoilage are estimated to be 30% to 40% of what is produced (FAO, 2013a; Godfray et al., 2010; Foley et al., 2011; Cassidy et al., 2013; DEFRA, 2012).

RESOURCE AND POPULATION DISTRIBUTIONS

As discussed above, food production and population are factors relevant to food security. Also relevant is their distribution—that is, on the local, regional and global scale, whether food distribution is well matched to population distributions. In some cases, such as war zones, it can be extremely difficult to get sufficient food to where people are. However, even in peaceful population-dense areas it can prove challenging, particularly in countries without food abundance and with poor infrastructure. One of the motives for local and urban agriculture is to grow food closer to where people are, and the goal of "smart" distribution systems and supply chains is to deliver food more effectively to where it is needed.

SOCIAL AND POLITICAL INSTITUTIONS

As the poverty, utilization and distribution factors indicate, food insecurity is not always, or even usually, due to limitations in food production or even in food availability. It is often a matter of food *access*. It is about people having the physical, social and economic resources or *capabilities* to secure food for themselves and their families. Social, political and economic institutions and policies are enormously influential on people's capabilities with respect to food security. They empower some actors over others, change incentive structures, set mandates, open and close markets, impact food prices, alter technology availability, create conflicts, affect ecological systems, displace people, and impact incomes. Here are just a few examples of innumerable cases of this:

- Subsidies for fertilizer and seed are associated with increases in food production in less developed countries.
- In the United States, the prevalence of corn is in part due to government subsidies and biofuel mandates. Moreover, by making corn feed less expensive, these subsidies prop up industrialized meat production. In South America and Europe, biofuel mandates affect the utilization of agricultural lands and products—i.e. which crops are grown and whether calories enter the food supply.
- National and international trade policies, tariffs, loans and aid agreements often impact the types of agriculture in developing nations—e.g. polyculture or commodity—as well as whether food is consumed domestically or shipped elsewhere.
- Land policies and international trade/investment agreements are relevant to the prevalence of bulk land acquisitions, sometimes called *land grabs*, where investors (governmental or private) purchase large amounts of agricultural land. Between 2000 and

2010, approximately 70 million hectares were sold or leased in developing nations, over 56 million of which were in Africa, representing nearly 5% of its agricultural land. Acquired lands are predominantly used for commodities, animal feed and fuel crops, and often involve the displacement of local farmers (World Watch Institute, 2012).

- Minimum wage and compensation laws are relevant to whether people can afford nutritionally adequate food. For example, in the United States, full-time minimum wage workers earn less than the national poverty line. Notably, food assistance programs are available to those earning up to 185% of the poverty line.
- Local, national and international welfare and food assistance programs affect whether poor people are able to meet their nutritional needs when they cannot pay market prices.
- Environmental and labor regulations are relevant to whether food costs can be made lower by externalizing ecological and human health impacts.
- Immigration and visiting worker laws affect remittances to developing countries, which are now three times the amount of official development assistance.
- Patent laws affect access to agricultural and food processing technologies, such as seed and machinery.
- Regulatory and food safety laws affect food system structures. For example, in the United States, GM crops are almost exclusively commercialized by large corporations in part due to the high costs for gaining regulatory approval, and one reason that food processing has become highly centralized is the cost associated with meeting regulatory standards.

The factors that impact food availability and security are not discrete, but highly interrelated. Social and economic policies, institutions and practices are particularly important in this regard, since they affect everything from food production to trade to poverty to fertility rates. However, it is true of the other factors as well. For example, productivity increases are often associated with price reductions, which increase the capability of people to secure food, and technological innovation and dissemination often increase productivity. The crucial point is that food insecurity is not an inevitable situation that we can do nothing about, and it is not only the result of population growth and finite planetary resources. It is the product of several factors, many of which we can change.

ADDRESSING GLOBAL FOOD INSECURITY

Once the factors that are relevant to food access and food insecurity are understood, the possibilities for addressing global malnutrition become clear.

REDUCE POPULATION

Population is not the only factor relevant to food security, but it is a very significant one. Accomplishing fertility rates near replacement levels would result in nearly 10 billion fewer people in 2100 than the UN's high fertility scenario that projects almost 17 billion people. The global fertility rate has been declining for decades. In 1960, it was 4.92 births per woman; in 2011, it was 2.41. It has dropped in both highly industrialized nations and in less developed nations. Nearly half of the world's population now lives in nations with fertility rates below replacement levels. It is of course possible to dramatically reduce fertility rates by placing severe restrictions on the number of children that women can have, as was done in China where the fertility rate dropped from 5.86 in 1965 to 1.58 in 2011. However, there are also several highly effective and non-coercive approaches to reducing population:

- *Economic development*—Fertility rates are inversely related to national per capita incomes. Many industrialized nations, including Japan, most countries in Europe, the United States, Brazil, Australia, Taiwan and Singapore, have fertility rates below replacement levels (CIA, 2014). Raising incomes, particularly for those in lower deciles, not only increases the capability of people to purchase food now, it reduces the number of people in the future (Myrskyla et al., 2009).
- *Opportunities for women*—There is a strong correlation between educational attainment for women and fertility rates. The longer women stay in school, the fewer children they tend to have over the course of their lifetime. As the percentage of girls enrolled in secondary school begins to exceed 80%, national

average fertility rates decrease to below replacement levels. Similarly, the more workforce, professional and civic opportunities that women have, the lower the fertility rates will be (World Bank, 2011; Reading, 2011).

- *Access to health care*—There is a strong relationship between access to health care and lower fertility rates, particularly when health-care access results in decreased infant mortality. When infant mortality rates (the number of children who die before 1 year of age per 1,000 live births) decrease to approximately 3.0, fertility rates decrease to around replacement levels (World Bank, 2011; UN, 2009).

- *Access to family planning*—There is a strong relationship between access to contraception and fertility rates. In developing nations, this has been demonstrated by both natural and controlled experiments. For example, the fertility rate in Pakistan is over a child more (3.3) than in Bangladesh (2.2), where contraception is more widely available; and an intervention in part of Bangladesh in the 1970s and 1980s resulted in a drop in fertility rates of nearly two children per woman when contraception was made available (Ezeh et al., 2012; Cleland et al., 2006).

Overall, there is a strong record of dramatic reductions in fertility rates, across cultural and socio-political contexts, when women have improved access to employment outside the home, economic opportunity, education, health care, and family planning. Pursuing these goals (which needs to be done in context-specific and culturally-sensitive ways) is a win-win. They are ethically good in their own right, since they increase women's autonomy, promote equality, and improve human welfare and life outcomes, and they also reduce population and thereby help to meet the challenge of realizing global food security.

INCREASE PRODUCTIVITY

The "traditional" route to growing the food supply has been to convert more land to agriculture and to increase wild catch. However, this is no longer feasible. Most usable land has already been appropriated (and to bring in what remains would have enormous detrimental impacts on biodiversity), and almost all global fisheries are fully accessed (or over-accessed). As a result, productivity increases must be sought in other ways. As discussed earlier, food production per hectare has been increasing for decades. Nevertheless, there remains a sizeable gap between what many agricultural systems currently produce and what they could produce. For example, increasing nitrogen availability can increase production in organic agriculture. Improved irrigation and fertilizer use can increase production in polyculture. Greater crop rotation and use of cover crops can increase productivity in industrial agriculture. In general, improved capital availability, technology, seeds, soil conservation, and pest control techniques can increase yields. How to close yield gaps and increase yield potentials effectively, sustainably, and in ways that decrease food insecurity are highly context-specific. What will benefit smallholder subsistence polyculture in developing countries is different from what will increase yields for conventional commodity agriculture in industrialized countries. In both cases, however, dramatic yield increases are possible. For example, a review of intervention projects focused on smallholding farms in 57 poor countries found that yield increases above 50% are readily achievable, along with a reduction in pesticide use and gains in water efficiency (Pretty et al., 2006). A recent study of 16 staple crops (barley, cassava, groundnut, maize, millet, potato, oil palm, rapeseed, rice, rye, sorghum, soybean, sugarbeet, sugarcane, sunflower and wheat) found that increasing their productivity to 95% of their maximum yield, primarily by means of improved water and nutrient management, could increase global yields by 58% (and at 75% productivity, the yield gain would be 28%) (Foley et al., 2011). Another study, focused on rice, wheat and maize, found that global yield increases of 45% to 70% are possible from closing the yield gap while also reducing nutrient overuse (Mueller et al., 2012). Moreover, as already discussed, innovations in technology and farming practices can increase what is considered "maximum yield." Thus, it appears that there remains quite a lot of room for sustainable productivity gains.

CHANGE UTILIZATION PATTERNS

As discussed above, public policies and economic incentives have resulted in quite a lot of cultivated land shifting from food crop production to feed and fuel crop production. Between 2000 and 2010, the amount of cropland dedicated to biofuel production more than quadrupled. The shift has been particularly dramatic in the United States and Brazil, but is occurring in Africa and Asia as well. Also, as discussed above, the use of crops for animal feed, as opposed to direct human consumption, is highly inefficient. Thus, one way to dramatically increase food availability is to increase direct human consumption of calories and nutrition. A recent analysis found that the amount of calories available to the food system could be increased by up to 70%, enough to feed 4 billion people a diet of 2,700 kcal/day, just by shifting utilization in these ways. Even if only half of the crop calories fed to animals and used for fuel were to go to direct human consumption, 2 billion additional people could be fed at current levels of productivity. This would also leave pasture available for animal agriculture, which uses 26% of the Earth's land. The potential gains in *people nourished per hectare* are particularly high in biofuel- and meat-intensive regions. In India, 89% of crop calories are directly consumed by people, in China and Brazil it is approximately 45%, and in the United States only 27% of calories (and 14% of protein) produced by crops are directly consumed by people. Together, these four countries are responsible for nearly 50% of the crop calories grown globally (Cassidy et al., 2013).

REDUCE WASTAGE

The FAO estimates that a third of the food produced for human consumption is lost to wastage globally. This amounts to 1.3 billion tons of food annually, with an economic cost of approximately $750 billion USD (FAO, 2013a). Wastage occurs at all points in the food life cycle: agricultural production, post-harvest handling and storage, processing, distribution, consumption, and disposal. However, the losses are differently distributed along the food supply chain in developed and developing nations. In less developed countries, the losses are predominantly at the production, transport and processing stages and are the result of spoilage and pests. This is primarily due to a lack of infrastructure, such as harvesting technologies, storage capacity, efficient transportation and refrigeration. There is very little wastage at the retail, preparation and consumption stages in less developed countries, since food abundance does not exist and the percentage of income spent on food is high. For example, in India 25.2% of household income is spent on food consumed at home, in China it is 26.9%, in Guatemala 37.9% and in Kenya 44.8% (USDA, 2014a). Households living in extreme poverty spend as much as 60–80% of their income on food (World Food Programme, 2012). In affluent nations, where there is food abundance and robust infrastructure, food expenditure as a percentage of household income is much lower. In the United States, only 6.6% of household income is spent on food consumed at home (and only 10% on food overall), in the UK it is 9.1% (and only 11.6% overall), in France 13.2%, and in Canada 9.6%. As a result, the majority of food wastage occurs at the consumption and retail stages, where fruits, vegetables and bakery items are the primary discards. In the UK, 15% of food and beverage purchases are wasted, at a cost of £12 billion per year (£480 per household) (DEFRA, 2012). In the United States, approximately 25% of consumers' food and beverage purchases are ultimately discarded, at a cost estimated to be between $1,265 USD to $2,275 USD annually for a family of four (Gunders, 2012). Over the entire food supply chain in the United States, 273 pounds of food/person/year is lost (Buzby and Hyman, 2012). There is thus an enormous amount of food to be "gained" by the food system through the elimination of food wastage. In many less developed countries, improving technology access, storage capacity, transportation, financing availability, and electricity are crucial. In affluent nations, wastage could be decreased by such things as reducing portion sizes, eliminating subsidies (thereby increasing the cost of food), and improving the accuracy of expiration dates.

REDUCE POVERTY AND CHANGE CONSUMPTION DISTRIBUTIONS

One of the primary barriers to food access is economic. Many malnourished people live in places where adequate food and nutrition are available, but they cannot afford it. Thus, one way to reduce food insecurity is to improve poor people's economic condition or decrease the cost of food for them. This has been accomplished to a considerable extent in China, for example, where economic growth has accompanied dramatic declines in both poverty and child malnutrition rates since 1990. (As discussed earlier, poverty contributes to malnutrition, and malnutrition helps to perpetuate poverty.) However, economic growth alone does not ensure that poverty rates decline. Growth needs to reach those at the lower end of the economic distribution. This can be a challenge, since people in extreme poverty often lack the capabilities and opportunities, such as social and economic capital, secondary education, health care, mobility and technology, which enable participation in growing economies. Thus, in order for growth to have a large impact on food insecurity, it needs to be widespread.

It is also possible to increase food access in the absence of economic growth by decreasing economic inequality. As discussed earlier, the poorest 20% of the Earth's population have only 1% of the world's income, while the wealthiest 20% have 83% of the world's income. Programs and policies that address economic inequality or promote a decent minimum standard of living for everyone can increase people's ability to secure adequate calories and nutrition. (As discussed above, they can also reduce fertility rates.) There are examples of this in both developed and developing countries. In the United States, despite an enormous abundance of food, 17.6 million households (14.5%) and 49 million citizens (including 8.3 million children) were food insecure in 2012, with 7 million households reporting that they ate less food than they would have liked because they lacked the economic or social resources to secure it (USDA, 2014c). That so many people are food insecure in a country with so much food is the result of enormous economic inequality and the absence of robust social support systems, which are in turn the product of public policies regarding education, labor, health care, taxes and welfare. In most other affluent nations, there is very little food insecurity. Such things as strong public assistance programs, progressive tax rates, living wage laws, universal health care and equitably funded education systems ensure a higher decent minimum quality of life and pull against dramatic inequality.

With respect to less developed nations, there are regions with comparatively low per capita economic activity that also have low food insecurity. One of the most prominently cited examples of this is Kerala, India, where there have been large increases in quality of life outcomes—improved educational achievement, more widespread civic participation, decreased infant mortality rates, and significant poverty reduction—despite limited economic growth. This has been largely attributed to efforts to reduce social and political inequality, as well as to foster a more equitable distribution of resources (e.g. education and health care). In contrast to Kerala, many other parts of India, with similar per capita economic activity but with greater social and political inequality, have much higher poverty rates and more food insecurity, as well as lower literacy rates and higher infant mortality rates.

Thus, it is possible to reduce food insecurity and address malnutrition with economic growth, more equitable distribution of economic resources, and direct assistance. Assistance and redistribution can be either domestic or international. A recent World Bank analysis estimated the global aggregate poverty gap—i.e. the amount of money that would be required to bring everyone up to the very low poverty line of $1.25 USD ppp/day—to be $169 billion USD (Olinto et al., 2013), while an analysis by the Brookings Institution put it at only $66 billion USD (Chandy and Gertz, 2011). Closing the gap would cost more than this, since it is not possible to perfectly target the resources at zero cost, and accomplishing food security will often require that people have more than $1.25 USD ppp/day on which to live. But these figures do give us a sense of the amount required.

Taken together, the foregoing indicates the tremendous potential for achieving sustainable food security. Despite the scale of the problem, it seems an achievable goal. Moreover, many people and organizations are doing the hard work of developing, implementing and evaluating specific, context-appropriate strategies, technologies, programs and policies for realizing each of these avenues for increasing food security.

NATIONAL OBLIGATIONS

It is possible to dramatically decrease malnutrition and food insecurity. The ethical question, for those of us in affluent nations, is whether we have a responsibility to use our resources to help do so. We can ask this at both the national and individual levels. In this section, I discuss whether affluent nations have a responsibility to address global malnutrition. In the following section, I discuss whether individuals have a responsibility to do the same.

THE ETHICAL CASE FOR ASSISTANCE

There are several ethical considerations offered in support of affluent nations helping to address global food insecurity. The primary of these is simple *compassion*. There are a wide variety of conditions and experiences that are considered "suffering." The experience of physical injury and emotional anguish differ dramatically, for instance. But what they have in common—what makes them suffering—is their unpleasantness and undesirableness. Thus, suffering, by definition, is bad and (all other things being equal), it is better if there is less of it. To be compassionate is to be moved by the suffering of others to act in ways that acknowledge and alleviate it. Caloric and micronutrient deficiencies cause tremendous suffering. Affluent nations with excess economic and food resources are aware of the suffering involved in extreme poverty and malnourishment, and are in a position to help alleviate that suffering. Therefore, the compassionate thing to do is to provide assistance.

A second ethical consideration offered in support of assisting those who are chronically malnourished is *human rights*. International statements on human rights are clear in stating that people have a right to basic sustenance and the minimum resources needed to be healthy. For example, the Universal Declaration of Human Rights asserts (Article 25): "Everyone has the right to a standard of living adequate for the health and well-being of himself and of his family, including food, clothing, housing and medical care and necessary social services, and the right to security in the event of unemployment, sickness, disability, widowhood, old age or other lack of livelihood in circumstances beyond his control" (UN, 1948). Moreover, many other internationally recognized rights, from self-determination to access to the benefits of science and technology (UN, 1966), presuppose food security. It is difficult for people to exercise their rights, or to advocate for them, when they are suffering from chronic malnutrition and occupied with trying to feed their families. National statements of individual rights also often include access to basic resources for life and health, and the constitutions of many countries, such as Brazil, Guatemala, Cuba, Iran and South Africa, explicitly include a right to food.

In addition to nationally and internationally recognized *legal rights*, many believe that people have a *moral right* to adequate nutrition. This right involves not having others act in ways that prevent you from meeting your basic needs (often called "*negative rights*"), as well as having the capabilities to pursue and satisfy these needs (often called "*positive rights*"). Moral rights are thought to be grounded in the value (or dignity) of people or to follow from the recognition that we cannot reasonably expect to have our basic needs protected and met without recognizing that we have the same responsibility to others. There is nothing exceptional about ourselves that justifies differential standing or protection.

A third ethical consideration offered in support of national assistance is *justice*. There are several different but interrelated bases for the claim that affluent nations should address global poverty and malnutrition as a duty of justice. The *historical argument* points out that in many places where there is significant food insecurity affluent nations contributed to creating this situation through their past activities, namely, colonialism, the forced appropriation of resources, the slave trade, the establishment of national boundaries, involvement in armed conflict, and the installation of governments. The claim is not that all food insecurity is the result of the past actions of affluent nations or that, where it is a cause, it is the primary or sole cause. The claim is that in parts of Africa, Asia, Latin America, the Caribbean and the Middle East the exercise of external military, economic and political power was a significant contributing factor to the ecological, social and economic conditions that gave rise to the problem of food insecurity in those places.

The *international order argument* for assistance is based on the fact that international institutions are largely set up and dominated by powerful affluent nations, which frequently promote policies that serve their own economic and geopolitical interests to the disadvantage of less developed nations. This charge is commonly made regarding economic institutions, such as the World Bank, the International Monetary Fund and the World Trade Organization, whose policies and agreements have significant impacts on trade, economic development, property ownership, agriculture and debt in the developing world. According to this argument, if international organizations, agreements and arrangements (regarding things as diverse as arms sales and intellectual property protections) benefit countries that are already well off to the disadvantage of those that are worst off, then affluent nations owe a debt of justice to less developed nations.

The *shared benefits argument* for a responsibility of assistance is based on the claim that affluent nations benefit from the economic position of less developed nations in numerous ways—e.g. by having access to inexpensive labor, purchasing their natural resources (from timber to rare earth elements), buying their land, externalizing environmental costs (e.g. electronic waste), and coercing them (e.g. through the terms of loans and aid) to open their markets and commodify their agriculture. If affluent nations benefit from the poverty of less developed nations, then justice requires that they share the benefits with them. Contributing to the alleviation of poverty and malnutrition is a crucial aspect of doing so, be it by direct wealth transfer or promoting technology access and economic development. Thus, there are thought to be historical, structural and benefits-sharing bases for the claim that justice requires affluent nations to address global poverty and malnutrition.

A fourth ethical consideration offered in support of a responsibility of assistance is *moral luck*. Moral luck is based on the idea that no one deserves the situation that they are born into. The reason for this is that prior to conception people do not exist, and if they do not exist they cannot have done anything to deserve anything. So it is just a matter of luck (and not desert) that some people are born into a situation of affluence while other people are born into a situation of extreme poverty. Moreover, among the greatest predictors of people's economic outcomes over the course of their lives—both within countries and between countries—are the socioeconomic situation into which they are born and whether they are male or female (something else people have no control over). There are several commonly accepted normative principles, based on the equal worth of people, on which this situation is problematic: A person should get what they deserve and deserve what they get; All people should have an equal opportunity at social and economic success; and All people should be socially and economically equal unless there is a good reason for inequality. None of these principles imply that there must be equality of outcome—i.e. that people should end up with roughly the same social and economic results. They allow for inequalities on the condition that there is some good justification for them—e.g. that they are earned, beneficial even to those who are less well off, or increase social welfare overall. Because the undeserved starting positions involved in the "natural lottery" of birth do not satisfy these conditions, there is a responsibility to address them. At a minimum, this involves assisting those who are born into extreme poverty as a matter of dumb luck to achieve the amount of nutrition required for normal development and health.

OBJECTIONS AND REPLIES TO THE CASE FOR NATIONAL ASSISTANCE

The considerations discussed above are intended to justify the view that affluent nations have an ethical obligation to use some of their resources to assist people who are chronically undernourished. Several considerations have been raised against such a responsibility.

Perhaps the best-known argument against affluent nations sending food aid to developing nations is Garrett Hardin's *lifeboat ethic*. Hardin suggested that we think of each country as a lifeboat, with a limited amount of space (or carrying capacity) defined by its resource base. Countries with high rates of poverty and malnutrition have more people than they are able to support; they are over capacity. This is a terrible situation, and it is understandable that some nations might want to send aid (or let people into their own country via immigration). However, in Hardin's view doing so would only make matters worse. For one thing, it would enable further population growth, increasing the number of people in "over-capacity" countries and thereby the number of people suffering. It would also deplete the capacity of the other countries to provide for their own citizens and protect resources for nonhuman species. Moreover, it would function as a disincentive for countries to take steps to address the causes of their resource and population problems. The end result of direct food assistance, on this view, will be unabated growth in population and depletion of resources and biodiversity until there is, finally, a dramatic ecological and population collapse. Therefore, although not sending aid may seem callous, it is the lesser of two bad scenarios: providing aid would only make matters much worse in the long run for both people and nature.

Some aspects of Hardin's view have merit. For example, it is sensitive to the fact that international institutions and policies are relevant to population, poverty and malnutrition, and that they frequently impact national policies. It recognizes that we need to reserve resources for nonhuman species. And, of course, population is a significant factor in global poverty and malnutrition. Nevertheless, critics argue, the lifeboat ethic is a misrepresentation of the international situation, and it makes false assumptions about how to effectively reduce population, poverty and malnutrition. Regarding the lifeboat analogy itself, nations are not independent entities with discrete resources that define their carrying capacities. They are deeply interconnected and interdependent with respect to natural resources, labor, food, and more; this is the distinctive feature of globalization. Moreover, as discussed earlier, poverty is actually associated with higher fertility rates. Fertility rates in less developed countries are reduced by decreasing poverty, increasing access to health care and family planning, and promoting educational and employment opportunities for women. Direct food aid alone would not accomplish this, but more comprehensive assistance, including agricultural programs, can (FAO, 2012b). Therefore, the lifeboat ethic appears to be wrong on the facts. Assistance in the right form reduces poverty and malnutrition. This point applies as well to the argument that providing food aid is not sustainable and will promote dependency. Even if this is true regarding providing only direct food aid, it is not applicable to a more comprehensive approach focused on education, health care, technology and economic development, or (perhaps) to one involving direct monetary assistance that allows people to spend resources on what they most need.

A second argument sometimes raised against a responsibility of national assistance is that international aid will be ineffective due to the dysfunction of governments in developing nations, or that it empowers despotic leaders and regimes by providing them leverage (i.e. via food provision) over their people and by forestalling public opposition to them. This may be true in some cases. There may be some countries where the regimes in power are so dysfunctional or corrupt, or the situation is so unstable, that aid of the sort described above would be ineffective or even problematic. However, most countries are not like this, and many aid programs, by national governments as well as by international institutions, have standards for governance, transparency and stability that must be met for aid eligibility.

A third argument often raised against a responsibility of national assistance is that the situation in which impoverished countries find themselves is of their own making. Therefore, it is their responsibility to address their own problems. The primary responses to this view have already been discussed. The justice argument belies the claim that affluent nations are not at all responsible for global poverty and malnutrition. The moral luck argument shows that individual poor and malnourished people typically are not primarily responsible for the situation they are in. The compassion argument aims to show that affluent nations ought to help those suffering from chronic malnutrition because they are in a position to do so, regardless of how the situation came about.

A fourth argument sometimes raised against providing assistance is that the cost of doing so is too high. However, the global poverty gap—the amount required to raise everyone to the global poverty line—is only a few hundred billion dollars per year (as mentioned above). This is a very small fraction of the gross domestic income (GDI) of affluent nations. Global economic activity (total gross domestic product (GDP) for all nations) in 2012 was approximately $72 trillion USD (World Bank, 2014c). The European Union's GDP alone was approximately $17 trillion USD and the United States' was approximately $16 trillion USD. In 2012, the official development assistance (ODA) of the members of the Organization for Economic Co-operation and Development (OECD) was only 0.29% of gross national income (GNI), approximately $125 billion USD. For the United States, it was 0.19% and for the UK it was 0.56%. In fact, only five countries met the United Nations' goal of 0.7%—Denmark, Luxemburg, Norway, Netherlands and Sweden (OECD, 2013a). In comparison, global military expenditures in 2012 were approximately $1.6 trillion USD, 39% (approximately $625 billion USD) of which was by the United States. Thus, the resources exist to address global food insecurity and poverty, and the costs to developed nations would in fact be quite low.

The information above belies a fifth argument against the ethical argument for increasing international assistance, namely, that affluent nations should prioritize helping their own citizens. It is possible to do both at comparatively modest cost—e.g. relative to military expenditures. In fact, affluent nations do prioritize their own citizens. Even the United States, which has large numbers of people who are food insecure, spends more on domestic food assistance programs ($75 billion USD) than on international food aid ($2.3 billion USD). It should also be noted that the predominant form of international food aid is exporting food grown in the United States, via U.S.-flagged ships, rather than providing cash grants and technology transfers to help enable food-insecure nations to develop their agricultural capacities, a much more efficient and effective long-term strategy.

A sixth argument often made against a responsibility of national assistance is that this is a problem that should be left to the market, which is more efficient at distributing resources than are governments. There is a kernel of truth to this argument: increased economic activity is associated with a decrease in malnutrition. However, market mechanisms are not maximally effective at ensuring that everyone's nutritional needs are met. We have seen that many people go hungry where food is available because they cannot afford it, that market (or price) volatility is a significant contributor to food insecurity, that the market (influenced by policy choices) can favor shifting agricultural resources to fuel and feed crops, and that there is an enormous amount of food loss and wastage. Free and open markets are highly efficient for getting resources and food to where they are most economically valuable, but market forces appear to have significant limitations when it comes to accomplishing resource utilization, distribution and access that promote global food security.

Finally, a seventh argument sometimes raised against assistance is that while it would be ethically good for affluent nations to address global poverty and malnutrition, they do not have an obligation to do so. This is how many people think about charity. It is good to volunteer to help others and make donations to charitable organizations. It is ethically better to do these things than to spend time playing video games and to spend money on designer shoes. However, it is not *wrong* to refrain from doing them. After all, people have a right to use their time and resources how they like. Perhaps this is how we ought to think of international assistance. It is ethically preferable for countries to shift resources from their militaries, for example, to addressing global malnutrition and poverty, but it is not wrong if they do not do so.

Whether something is ethically required or merely ethically good depends upon the justification for doing it, as well as the costs involved. If the justification is very strong—i.e. if there are extremely important things at stake and/or the justification appeals to one's own role in creating an ethically problematic situation—it pulls toward obligation. With respect to food insecurity, the welfare of 842 million people is at stake, and several of the arguments for assistance appeal to the role of affluent nations in creating, perpetuating and benefiting from this situation. Thus, the types of considerations involved in the arguments for a responsibility of national assistance suggest that it would not only be good for affluent nations to assist food-insecure nations, but it would be wrong for them not to, particularly given that the costs of providing assistance to them appears to be relatively low.

INDIVIDUAL OBLIGATIONS

If affluent nations have a responsibility to address the problem of food insecurity, they are not meeting it. This invites the following question: Do individuals have a responsibility to try to help?

THE CORE ARGUMENT FOR INDIVIDUAL RESPONSIBILITY

It is a common view that people have a responsibility to help others in dire situations when they are in a position to do so and the costs of helping are not too high. If you are walking past a park and there is a child who is drowning in a pond, you have an obligation to assist him, even if it will cost you some resources—e.g. it will ruin your new clothes or make you late for work. Not helping a drowning child on the grounds that it will cost you $150 USD in pay or clothing would be wrong, most people would agree.

The most influential ethical argument for an individual obligation to address global malnutrition is that the same considerations that hold in the drowning child scenario also apply to donating money (or time and effort) to famine relief and international assistance organizations. You can help to prevent the suffering or death of a child, and (for most of us in affluent nations) the cost of doing so is not very high. Four hundred million children live in extreme poverty, and in some parts of the world child malnutrition rates exceed 30%. More than 100 million children are undernourished and underweight globally, and 1 in 4 children show signs of stunting. Micronutrient deficiencies can lead to serious diseases and death; and the global poor are exposed to elevated rates of pathogens and parasites (UN, 2013b). Estimates differ, but it appears that for most children living in extreme poverty $150 is more than enough to deliver vaccinations, provide basic health care, and close the nutritional gap between the crucial ages of 2 and 5—and in 2012, 6.6 million children died before the age of 5 (UNICEF, 2013b). Thus, a $150 USD donation to a reputable aid organization is enough to help save the life of a child.

The *core argument in favor of individual assistance*, then, is this:

(1) If you can prevent something very bad from happening with little cost to yourself, then you should do so.
(2) Child poverty and malnutrition are very bad, due to the suffering and, sometimes, death involved.
(3) Even modestly affluent people can prevent some child poverty and malnutrition with little cost to themselves by donating a relatively small amount of money (or time and effort) to reputable aid organizations.
(4) Therefore, people with the means to do so ought to donate to reputable aid organizations.

This argument is frequently buttressed by other ethical considerations discussed earlier: justice, human rights and moral luck.

OBJECTIONS AND REPLIES TO THE CASE FOR INDIVIDUAL ASSISTANCE

There are several common objections to the argument for an individual responsibility to contribute to malnutrition reduction efforts. Each one focuses on a difference between the pond scenario and sending aid. The replies to these objections argue that those differences are either only apparent or not ethically significant. Here are the most frequently proffered differences and the responses to them.

1. *In the pond case, you are physically and socially close to the victim, whereas in the aid case you are not.* One difference between the two cases is distance, both spatial and social (or cultural). But why should how far away you are from the person you could help matter? Suppose that instead of walking by the pond, you are all the way on the other side of the park when a person (who cannot swim) runs up to you in a panic and asks you (because you can swim) to help save a child in the pond. To say "I would

help if the pond were here, but not if I have to go all the way over there" seems ethically problematic precisely because it takes something as relevant—physical distance—which is not relevant. To respond by saying "Is the person someone I know?" or "Is the person the same nationality or ethnicity as me?" seems just as bad (or even worse), since it suggests that cultural (or social) similarity is ethically relevant, when it is not.

2. *In the pond case, you are saving one child, whereas with global malnutrition there are more children that you can help (i.e. the problem is just so much bigger).* "Ought implies can" is a widely accepted principle in ethics. It means that you cannot be obligated to do something that you are not capable of doing. You can save one drowning child, but you cannot end global malnutrition. Therefore, according to this response, you can be obligated in the pond case, but not the aid case. However, the core argument in favor of individual assistance does not claim that you have a responsibility to end malnutrition, only that you have a responsibility to help save a child (or as many children as you can reasonably afford to save). Moreover, the fact that you cannot save everyone does not imply that you should not try to save anyone. To accept that would be to commit *the perfectionist fallacy*, i.e. that if it is not possible to do something perfectly, then it is not worth doing it at all. Imagine that you are walking past a pond in which a boat has flipped over and in which several children are drowning—more children than you could save. So you say: "If it were only one child, I would definitely try to save him, but since there are more than I can save I am not going to try to save any." This response is problematic precisely because it commits the perfectionist fallacy. But it is essentially the same as the "too big a problem" response to sending aid.

3. *The pond case is a one-off event, whereas there are always people in need of food assistance.* One certainty about donating to international aid organizations is that if you give once, the requests will keep coming. However, imagine that you are walking past a pond in which a child is drowning and that you say: "I would definitely try to save that child, but I just saved one last month, so this time I am going to pass." It could be that repeatedly saving the life of children adds up in cost to the point that it significantly impacts your own welfare. But so long as it does

not, and the costs continue to be relatively small, then all the considerations that justified saving the child last month do so again this month. The same seems to apply to international assistance. So long as it is not adding up to a significant burden, the fact that you might be asked to assist again in the future seems irrelevant to whether you ought to help.

4. *In the pond case, you are the only one around, whereas there are lots of other people who could help send food aid (including governments).* Imagine that in the pond case, rather than walking alone, you are with your friends, one of whom is an emergency medical technician who works for the city. When you come across the drowning child, all of your companions, including the person whose job it is to help people in distress, refuse to save the child. This is terrible of them. But does the fact that they act in an ethically problematic way make it permissible for you to do so as well? Most people would think not. Our ethical responsibilities do not disappear just because other people fail to act well. Similarly, this response goes, the fact that others, including governments, could assist those suffering from malnutrition does not mean that we do not have a responsibility to assist them.

5. *In the pond case, you know that your resources are going toward trying to save a child, whereas in the aid case there is much greater uncertainty.* In the pond case, you are the one who makes the effort to save the child. In the aid case, you send your resources off for others to use (unless you volunteer in ways that involve more direct assistance). This adds some uncertainty. However, there are established and reliable aid organizations, as well as independent organizations that evaluate their effectiveness and monitor their expenditures. If resources are sent to the right places, there can be high confidence that they will be used for their intended purpose. Moreover, there is some uncertainty even in the pond case. Perhaps you are unable to get there in time. If so, then your resources would be "wasted." Nevertheless, most people would think that you should still try to save the child. Furthermore, although you are the one who pulls the child from the pond, that is not the end of the aid. The child might then be evaluated, given medical assistance, and returned to parents or taken to social services. Thus, even in the pond case you do not complete the save on your own and you may not

be around to see how things turn out in the end. Still, you ought to try to do your part to help the child. So, the fact that there is some uncertainty and the fact that you are not the one directly delivering the aid in the malnutrition case do not make it very different from the pond case and do not appear ethically relevant (so long as the uncertainty is low enough) in any event.

6. *The cost of assistance in the pond case is only some ruined clothes or lost work, but in the aid case it is an amount of money that is significant to many people, even those in affluent nations.* It is certainly true that $150 USD is significant to some people in affluent nations, particularly those in or near poverty. However, proponents of the argument emphasize, the ethical responsibility is conditional on its fulfillment not being a hardship. Therefore, it does not apply to people in that situation. Moreover, for most people in affluent nations $150 USD is not a very large amount. We spend tens of billions of dollars on game apps for our phones each year and far more than that on shoes and clothing we do not need. We eat costly meals out, purchase expensive cars for the bells and whistles, take pricey trips during our vacations, and so on.

Each of these objections (except the last) to the core argument in favor of individual assistance aims to show that there is something about the aid case that is different and ethically relevant from the immediate assistance case (the pond case). The responses argue that the differences are not really ethically relevant or not differences at all. The factors discussed above might be part of the *psychological explanation* for why it is that people are more likely to assist in an immediate emergency situation than to send aid to help address global malnutrition. However, there is a distinction between a psychological explanation for why people behave as they do and an *ethical justification* for what they should do. Ethics concerns what people ought to do, which is often different from what people actually do. We can provide social and psychological explanations for why people lie to gain an advantage, act self-destructively, and treat other people badly. But the fact that we can offer explanations of these things does not make them ethically acceptable. So, while factors like distance, repeatability, scale, invisibility and uncertainty might explain people's reluctance to help address global malnutrition, that is different from their justifying it as ethically acceptable.

HOW MUCH TO GIVE?

Suppose there is an individual responsibility to help address global poverty and malnutrition. The next issues are how to help and how much of one's own resources to put toward it. (The focus of the discussion above and in what follows is wealth transfer or monetary donation, but the considerations discussed apply to time and effort as well—e.g. volunteering, career choices, organizing, and advocating for policy changes.) One crucial consideration is effectiveness—i.e. using resources in ways that efficiently address the problem now and in the future. The discussion earlier on the causes of malnutrition and the ways in which it could be addressed speak to this. There are several ethically attractive possibilities, many of which represent win-wins, such as reducing fertility rates and promoting economic development through increased access to health care and education for women. Precisely where to aim one's resources, which types of efforts and organizations to support and in what locations, is beyond the scope of this discussion. What is crucial is that they address the factors that give rise to the problem and that they do so effectively, efficiently, sustainably, and in ways that are not ethically problematic. There are many agricultural, financial, educational, health care, and other types of organizations and programs that satisfy these conditions.

How much to give is a bit more vexing. The principle suggested above was that *a person should give so long as it does not significantly impact her own welfare*. This means forgoing things that are trivial, mere preferences and luxuries, but it does not require diverting resources from things that are relevant to one's quality of life, such as health care and education. Peter Singer, who originally formulated the drowning child and international aid thought experiment, has at times proposed that an even stronger standard might be justified, that *one should give so long as the benefits of your assistance to others outweigh the costs to you*. This would mean that one should give just up to the point of becoming economically insecure oneself, which strikes many as far too demanding. Moreover, it depends upon the implausible idea that we should not put any more weight on our own welfare (or that of our family and friends) than that of a stranger. Another principle that has been proposed to describe the extent of the obligation of assistance is that people with more than adequate resources have *an obligation to do their fair share* to address global poverty and malnutrition. One way a fair share is sometimes defined is as an equal share or the amount that each person with adequate means would have to give to achieve global food security (or eliminate global poverty) if everyone gave the same amount. On this definition, and taking the top 1% of global earners as those with adequate means—i.e. those with incomes above approximately $34,000 USD per person in the household after taxes or $136,000 USD for a family of four (Milanovic, 2012)—this would amount to approximately $5,500/year USD per person (assuming $400 billion USD is needed, which is at the high end of estimates). A fair share is also sometimes defined relative to a person's overall income or wealth. On an "income-relative" share, the demand on most of the world's affluent people drops significantly, since the income and wealth of the super-rich are so great. The 2012 income of the 100 wealthiest people in the world was $240 billion USD, and the total net worth of the world's 1,645 billionaires is estimated to be $6.4 trillion USD (Kroll, 2014).

At present, donations from affluent individuals to international aid organizations fall far short of what is needed to address global malnutrition and close the global poverty gap. In the United States, for example, only approximately $19 billion USD was given to international aid organizations by individual donors in 2012, less than was spent on phone apps and cosmetic surgery. (Overall, United States citizens and foundations made over $300 billion USD in charitable contributions in 2012, approximately $100 billion USD of which went to religious organizations and approximately $80 billion USD of which went to domestic health and human services organizations.) By far the greatest contribution to "international aid" is the over $400 billion USD that migrant workers from developing countries send home each year, which is over three times the amount of official development assistance (World Bank, 2013; FAO, 2013c).

CONCLUSION

Malnutrition is among our greatest global challenges. The sheer numbers involved sometimes invite despair: How can we possibly feed over 7.2 billion people a nutritionally adequate and culturally appropriate diet in a sustainable way with our finite planetary resources, particularly when there is already over 800 million people who are chronically undernourished? However, the number of people suffering from malnutrition has actually fallen in recent years. Moreover, in the first half of this chapter we saw that there are ways to effectively reduce fertility rates by improving people's lives, ways to increase the food supply without expanding agriculture, ways to improve yields while reducing ecological impacts, and ways to increase food access by decreasing extreme poverty and increasing capabilities. The second half of this chapter focused on whether those of us who are affluent have an ethical responsibility, as nations and as individuals, to put some of our resources toward assisting those in serious need. I discussed the core argument for assistance, the most prominent objections to that argument, as well as responses to those objections. If there is a responsibility to assist, the extent to which we ought to contribute, as well as whether it is ethically obligatory or merely ethically good to do so, need to be determined.

FURTHER READING

Many of the books on food systems, food ethics and food justice listed in the Further Reading section of Chapter 1 discuss malnutrition and food insecurity, including potential strategies and responsibilities for addressing them. Some books that focus specifically on these issues are:

Peter Singer, *The Life You Can Save: Acting Now to End World Poverty* (Random House)

Thomas Pogge, *World Poverty and Human Rights* (Polity)

Amartya Sen, *Poverty and Famines: An Essay on Entitlement and Deprivation* (Oxford University Press)

Amartya Sen, *Development as Freedom* (Anchor)

Martha Nussbaum, *Creating Capabilities: The Human Development Approach* (Belknap)

Peter Unger, *Living High and Letting Die: Our Illusion of Innocence* (Oxford University Press)

Philip Cafaro and Eileen Crist, eds., *Life on the Brink: Environmentalists Confront Overpopulation* (University of Georgia Press)

SHOULD WE EAT ANIMALS?

People eat an estimated 146 billion nonhuman animals (hereafter just *animals*) each year, approximately 56 billion land animals and 90 billion aquatic animals. One of the most prominent topics in food ethics is whether eating animals is ethically acceptable. There are *a lot* of views on the issue. For example, *ethical vegetarianism* is the view that we ought not eat animals. *Ethical veganism* is the view that we should refrain from eating animals, as well as from eating (and using) animal products such as milk, cheese and leather. *Ethical pescetarianism* is the view that it is ethically permissible to eat fish, but not land animals. *Obligatory carnivorism* is the view that not only is it permissible to eat animals, it is obligatory for people to do so. *Ethical omnivorism* (or *compassionate carnivorism*) is the view that it is permissible to eat animals so long as they are treated humanely.

In the first half of this chapter, I discuss the two primary ethical arguments against eating agriculturally produced meat—*the argument from animal welfare* and *the argument from ecological impacts*—as well as several other considerations relevant to the ethics of animal consumption. In the second half of this chapter, I focus on the ethics of wild capture through hunting and fishing.

ARGUMENT FROM ANIMAL WELFARE

Many people are ethically opposed to eating meat on the grounds that it requires causing animals to suffer and die. Here is the core animal welfare argument against meat eating:

1. Animal agriculture causes very large amounts of suffering.
2. We ought not cause suffering to others without adequate reason.
3. There is no adequate reason for animal agriculture.
4. Therefore, we ought to adopt a non-meat diet.

Premise one—animal agriculture causes very large amounts of suffering—is an empirical claim. There are two components to it. The first is that nonhuman animals have the capacity to suffer or feel pain—i.e. they are *sentient*. The second is that the practices used in animal agriculture are painful to the animals involved.

The claim that animals are sentient is based on the same kind of physiological and behavioral evidence that justifies the view that other people feel pain. We cannot experience the pain of other people firsthand. The belief that other people are sentient is nevertheless justified by the fact that they have the same underlying physiology as we do—e.g. a neurological system—and exhibit the same behaviors that we do in situations that would cause us pain—e.g. they wince and report their discomfort. These same considerations hold for animals. Dogs, for example, recoil when hit or burned, and have a nervous system very similar to our own. Moreover, while they do not speak, they engage in communicative acts that express pain, such as whimpering or yelping when exposed to stimuli that would cause pain in us. It was once commonly thought that animals were not sentient. However, that view has been discredited by the physiological and behavioral evidence, as well as by evolutionary biology, which explains the common origins of human and animal nervous systems and provides an evolutionary explanation for pain sensations.

The claim that animal agriculture causes significant pain to animals is based on how animals are standardly treated in large-scale farming operations, particularly in concentrated animal feed operations. *Animal feed operation* refers to animal agriculture in which feed is brought to animals, rather than the animals ranging or grazing for food. *Concentrated animal feed operations* (CAFOs) are feed operations in which there is a high density and large number of animals in one location. CAFOs have become increasingly prominent since the second half of the twentieth century. They now produce the majority of meat consumed in the United States and are expanding elsewhere in the world. The U.S. Environmental Protection Agency (EPA) defines a large CAFO as one that has a minimum of 125,000 chickens, 82,000 egg-laying hens, 10,000 swine, 1,000 cattle for consumption, or 700 dairy cattle. However, they are often much bigger than this (EPA, 2014a).

CAFOs result from the features of industrialization (discussed in Chapter 1) being applied to animal agriculture—e.g. scale, efficiency, technologization, standardization, consolidation, specialization, minimization of input costs, and externalization of costs. For this reason, they are sometimes referred to, particularly by their critics, as *factory farms*. In CAFOs, animals are considered and treated as part of an industrial process to produce as much meat (or eggs or milk) as possible at as low a cost as possible. This, combined with the high concentration of animals, results in practices that cause suffering. For example, egg-laying hens are typically kept in rows and stacks of small "battery cages" that often do not allow them to stand or walk around. A large percentage of battery-caged birds have broken bones prior to slaughter. Chickens (and other fowl, such as turkey) are declawed and debeaked (without anesthesia) so that they do not harm each other and can be more easily handled. Swine are housed in individual gestation crates that are so small that they are not able to turn around. Breeding sows are often confined on their sides to make nursing more efficient. (Animal welfare concerns about gestation crates have led McDonald's and several other large purchasers of pork to require that their suppliers phase them out by 2020, and animal welfare concerns about battery cages have led to restrictions on their use in the European Union.) The tails of pigs are typically docked, and boars are castrated in order to improve the taste of pork. Dairy cattle are standardly given bovine growth hormones (BGH) and overfed in order to boost milk production. Reproduction is maximized through processes of artificial insemination, as soon as it is viable. Beef and dairy cattle are often fed corn-based diets, to which they are not well suited. Confinement of all animals prevents them from engaging in species-typical physical and social behaviors, and it requires the use of large amounts of antibiotics to prevent the spread of diseases. All of these are standard practices in CAFOs. While they are not practiced in every case, they are considered industry norms, and they are only a sampling of the treatments that result in animal suffering. In addition to these treatment issues, there are also serious and widespread concerns about stress and improper implementation of slaughter processes, which can result in live animals being boiled or butchered. Thus, the industrialization of animal agriculture results in large amounts of suffering.

Premise two—we ought not cause suffering to others without adequate reason—is based on the idea that suffering is bad for the one undergoing it. The view that suffering is bad for those experiencing it is not controversial. It is evidenced by the fact that people typically try to avoid suffering and to alleviate it when experiencing it. Moreover, as discussed in Chapter 2, it is built into the concept of suffering that it is bad or undesirable. There are a wide variety of sensations that we count as suffering—the felt experience of being left by one's partner is very different from that of breaking one's leg. What they have in common in virtue of which they are grouped together as "suffering" is just their undesirableness or unpleasantness. The fact that suffering is bad does not mean that it is always wrong to cause it in others. Going to the dentist sometimes involves quite a lot of pain and suffering, yet we should still bring our children there, since it is beneficial for them in the long run. To say that suffering is bad is not to claim that it is always wrong to cause it, *all things considered*. If there is a good enough reason, then it can be permissible (or even obligatory) to cause suffering. But the badness of suffering does imply that it should not be caused for trivial reasons or unnecessarily, particularly in the absence of the consent of the one undergoing it. It is not permissible to do painful dental work on others for fun, without their permission (or that of their guardian), or in ways that cause more pain than is needed.

Premise 3—there is no adequate reason for animal agriculture—is based on the fact that it is possible for most people to have a healthy diet without eating meat. There is in existence proof of this: the hundreds of millions of vegetarians who have lived long, healthy lives. It might be that some small number of people have a health need for protein from meat in particular, and there are people who live in situations where they depend upon meat as a food source (e.g. subsistence hunters and herders). However, for those who have access to adequate alternatives, meat eating is not necessary. It is something that people like to do—we have a preference for it—but it is not required to satisfy a basic or serious need. That a person has a preference for something is typically not considered adequate justification for causing others to suffer, particularly when their suffering is crucial to the satisfaction of the preference and they have not consented to it. It is not permissible to intentionally injure someone during a game because you want to win, for example. Therefore, for those of us who do not need to eat meat for our health or survival, there is no adequate justification for our contributing to animal suffering by doing so, according to this argument.

OBJECTIONS TO THE ARGUMENT FROM ANIMAL WELFARE

The animal welfare argument against eating meat has generated a great deal of discussion. In what follows, I review several objections to it and several responses to those objections.

LIMITED SCOPE

The animal welfare argument only shows that certain types of agricultural practices are ethically problematic, namely, those associated with large-scale industrial agriculture. The argument does not apply to traditional herding, pasturing, or free-range animal agriculture. These forms of animal agriculture can be done in ways that are adequately attentive to animal welfare. Moreover, the argument does not apply to hunting (when it is done in ways that minimize animal suffering) or to animals accidentally killed on roadways, for example. In addition, as is recognized in the argument itself, it does not apply to people who do not have ready access to nutritionally adequate non-meat diets. Therefore, the argument from welfare does not warrant the conclusion that people ought not eat meat. At best, it warrants the conclusion that people who have adequate alternatives ought not eat meat produced by CAFOs.

Because the argument from animal welfare trades on the suffering caused by animal agriculture, if there are forms of it that do not cause unnecessary suffering then they would not be subject to this argument (as the objection notes). However, some proponents of the animal welfare argument have pointed out that the alternatives cited in the response are not always so innocuous as they seem. There often are confinement, mistreatment, exposure and slaughtering problems (particularly when done by people who are not professionals) in alternative animal agriculture, for example. Still, one common response to the limited scope objection is to acknowledge that the conclusion only applies to meat produce in suffering-causing ways and to people who have adequate alternatives, while emphasizing that this is most of the meat in many places and most of the people in affluent nations.

Another response sometimes made to the limited scope objection is to shift the argument from an animal-suffering argument to an animal-killing and animal-use argument. Animals arguably have an interest both in not suffering and in not being killed, which is an essential part of all animal agriculture. If the problem is not just the suffering, but the killing and use of animals for our ends, particularly when not necessary, then the argument will apply to more humane forms of animal agriculture. This move is often associated with an *animal rights* view on the moral status of animals, as opposed to an *animal welfare* view. On an animal rights view, animals ought to be treated as ends in themselves, as mattering in and of themselves, and not merely as tools or means for our benefit. Thus, "cleaning up" animal agriculture by reducing suffering does not address the deeper problem, which is that we see and treat animals as mere things or objects for our use. That is, the problem with animal agriculture is not how it is done, but that it is done.

MEAT EATING IS NOT A MERE PREFERENCE

The animal welfare argument assumes that the only adequate justification for eating meat is that it is necessary for survival and health, and that all other reasons are mere wants. However, many people have more than just a peripheral interest in eating meat.

It can have special cultural significance, particularly when it is connected to ethnic, national and religious practices and celebrations. Moreover, many people are invested in culinary practices involving meat in ways that are not mere passing interests. It can be part of their work (e.g. chef, slaughterhouse worker, or feedlot owner) or a project in which they are deeply invested (e.g. food aesthetics and appreciation). Therefore, the argument is much too quick to classify all nonessential meat production and eating as "mere preferences."

RESPONSES TO MEAT EATING IS NOT A MERE PREFERENCE

Proponents of the animal welfare argument offer several responses to the claim that meat eating is often not a mere preference. First, it is possible to be invested in food—to be a chef or a foodie—without eating or preparing meat (or meat from CAFOs). There is a lot to appreciate about non-animal-based foods. They can taste wonderful, and many chefs have careers in the food industry without using animal products or by using only humanely produced animal products. Second, while some meat eating might be culturally significant, the vast majority is not. Most meat is eaten in mundane or routine contexts, and not as part of holidays or special preparations. Moreover, there are typically non-meat-based ways to maintain cultural cuisines and traditions. In addition, appealing to cultural tradition (or one's job or hobby) is not sufficient justification for doing something that would otherwise be ethically problematic. We do not think that it is permissible to cause other people to suffer so long as we come from a long tradition of doing so, it enriches our lives, or we are making a living from it. (The issue of how much normative significance should be given to appeals to cultural practices and traditions is discussed at much greater length in Chapter 6.)

AGRICULTURAL ANIMALS WOULD NOT OTHERWISE EXIST

Agricultural animals were bred specifically to be used and consumed by people. Because they would not exist if they did not serve our purposes, it is permissible to use them for the ends for which they were created. This includes eating them.

It is true that agricultural animals would not exist if they were not useful to people. However, inferring from this to the conclusion that it is therefore permissible to do to them as we see fit conflates the explanation for why something exists with their moral status when they exist. This can be easily seen in the case of people. If someone has children in order to sell them for a profit, it does not follow that it is permissible to do so, even if the children would not have existed had they not been created for that purpose. This applies to animals as well. For example, that dogs bred for dog fighting would not otherwise exist does not imply it is permissible to make them fight each other.

ANIMAL SUFFERING IS NOT MORALLY SIGNIFICANT

The argument from animal welfare (and several of the responses above) assumes that all suffering is bad, whether it is human suffering or animal suffering. If animal suffering is not morally significant—if it is not something that we need to care about—then it does not follow from the fact that animals suffer that it is wrong for us to cause them to suffer. At best, then, the argument from animal welfare is incomplete, since it does not justify the claim that animal suffering is morally significant. Moreover, there are important differences between humans and animals that might be a basis for not considering their suffering the same as ours. For example, they are not our species, they are not rational in the ways that we are, they are not self-aware, and they cannot engage in reciprocal obligations or cooperative arrangements with us. Perhaps most importantly, they are not moral agents. They do not and could not care about the ethics of causing suffering to others, and they cannot be held morally responsible for their actions. When you remove humans from the farm, there is no longer any morally good or bad, right or wrong. Therefore, agricultural animals are beyond the reach of moral concern—ethics does not apply to them.

This objection claims that we need a reason to think that animal suffering is ethically significant and that the animal welfare argument does not provide it. However, a justification for the ethical significance of animal suffering has been provided—i.e. the arguments for the badness of suffering. Given that suffering is bad, the onus is not on the proponents of the argument from animal welfare to explain why we should take animal suffering into account, it is on the argument's opponents to explain why we should not.

The objection proposes several possible differences between humans and animals that could be grounds for not considering the suffering of animals: they are not our species, they are not rational, they are not self-aware, and they are not moral agents. However, each of these suggestions suffers from one of two problems: they are either not ethically relevant differences or they do not distinguish all humans from all animals (or both). For example, human infants and the severely mentally disabled are not rational, self-aware (in the sense of conceiving of themselves as distinct individuals), or moral agents in the same ways as healthy adult human beings. (And in the case of the severely mentally disabled, they are not even potentially these.) Therefore, if these are criteria for being *morally considerable*—for having one's interests (including one's suffering) matter—then human infants and the severely mentally disabled are not morally considerable. However, it is clearly not permissible to do whatever we like to them, and this implies that those criteria are not appropriate for distinguishing which individuals are morally considerable from which individuals are not.

Moreover, that animals are of a different species from us does not itself imply that we can treat them however we like. It is crucial to distinguish *factual differences* from *morally relevant differences*. There are a lot of factual differences between people. People are different heights, from different places, and have different skin colors. Some of the factual differences between people are even deep biological differences—e.g. some people have XX chromosomes while others have XY chromosomes. However, we have learned over time that stature, place of origin, race and sex are not morally significant differences. They are real factual differences, but they do not justify considering people's interests differently—i.e. they are not relevant to moral considerability. To take them as ethically relevant is therefore deeply problematic. It is racist or sexist, for example. So while it is true that animals are factually different from humans, and that these differences are biological, this alone is not sufficient to justify not taking their interests into account. To do so would be to commit a sort of *speciesism*. To see this, imagine that it turns out that what we think of as *Homo sapiens* is actually two distinct species that evolved independently to have the same physiological, psychological and cognitive capacities. It would be absurd to think that upon this discovery the individuals of each species would be justified in not considering the interests of the other species on those grounds. The fact that people's capacities and the interests they ground remain the same is what matters ethically, not their species membership. If this is right—i.e. if it is capacities and interests that are crucial to moral considerability—and animals are sentient and have an interest in not suffering, then their suffering ought to be taken into consideration. As Jeremy Bentham famously put it:

> It may one day come to be recognized that the number of legs, the villosity of the skin, or the termination of the os sacrum are reasons equally insufficient for abandoning a sensitive being to the same fate. What else is it that should trace the insuperable line? Is it the faculty of reason, or perhaps the faculty of discourse? But a full-grown horse or dog is beyond comparison a more rational, as well as a more conversable animal, than an infant of a day or a week or even a month old. But suppose they were otherwise, what would it avail? The question is not, Can they reason? nor Can they talk? but, Can they suffer?
>
> (1823, ch. 17, n. 122)

That animal suffering is properly regarded as ethically significant does not imply that we must treat animals the same way that we treat people. We do not need to give pigs the vote and send chickens to school. Just as we should treat infants differently from adults due to the factual differences between them, we should treat humans and animals differently. This applies to different types of animals as well. It might be that we need to take the interests of both cows and dolphins into consideration, but it would be wrong to release cows into the open water and to graze dolphins in open pasture. It is crucial to distinguish *consideration* from *treatment*. To claim that animals are morally considerable is to assert that their interests need to be taken into account. It is not to claim that they have the same interests as humans or that their interests can be promoted in the same way as those of humans. A good bovine life is different from a good human life, and humans have a broader range of interests than do cows (due to our more robust psychological and cognitive capacities), even if it is wrong to cause both humans and cows to suffer without good justification.

APPEAL TO INCONSEQUENTIALISM

One person giving up eating meat is not going to reduce animal suffering whatsoever. It is not as if there are particular animals assigned to particular people, such that if a person gives up eating meat their animal will be spared. Given this, that a person wants to eat meat and enjoys doing so seems sufficient reason for her doing it. Refraining from eating meat would decrease her pleasure, and it would not benefit any animals. It might be ethically better if there were not large amounts of animal suffering, and legislation to prevent or reduce it would be ethically good. But in the absence of systemic change, why should one individual make sacrifices when it will not make any difference? Her eating meat is inconsequential.

RESPONSES TO APPEAL TO INCONSEQUENTIALISM

The issue of inconsequentialism commonly arises with respect to large-scale collective action problems. When a problem is the cumulative result of the actions of a large number of people—e.g. global climate change—the contribution of any one individual is often insignificant to addressing it. The question is then raised: Why should a person make an effort or take on the costs to change her behavior, when it will not make a difference as to whether the problem is resolved?

Several responses to the problem of inconsequentialism have been proposed. One is that inconsequential reasoning is self-defeating. If everyone applied it, then problems would never get resolved (and attempts to address them would not even be made), particularly since the problem of inconsequentialism arises in the context of political action as well. For example, inconsequential reasoning applied to voting in national elections would lead each person to conclude that they should not cast a ballot. At a minimum, this response continues, everyone has to do their part to address collective action problems, since the only way to resolve them is through the cumulative effects of everyone's negligible contributions.

Another response appeals to complicity and integrity. Even if you alone cannot end animal suffering in agriculture, or even save some number of animals, you can avoid benefiting from animal suffering and thereby being complicit with it. This is a matter of integrity, particularly if you recognize that the practice is ethically problematic. If you believe that child labor is ethically problematic, but nevertheless knowingly purchase cheap shoes that are made with child labor because you like them, then you suffer from a lack of character and are benefiting from exploitation. The same applies to eating meat produced in ethically problematic ways.

Finally, the premise of the inconsequentialism objection—i.e. that each person's actions are inconsequential to reducing animal suffering—is often denied. One common way of doing this is by appeal to the possibility of cascading effects. By embracing a non-meat diet, you can demonstrate that it is viable and beneficial, thereby encouraging others to do the same. They, in turn, can set an example for others to follow, and so on.

HOW FAR DOES THE ARGUMENT FROM ANIMAL WELFARE EXTEND?

The discussion in the previous section focused on whether the argument from animal welfare is sound. If it is sound, another important issue is determining how far it extends. Here are several "dimensions" of the argument to consider in this respect.

- *Does the argument only apply to CAFOs or does it extend to smaller-scale and alternative forms of animal agriculture?* As discussed above, its extension along these dimensions largely depends upon the extent to which non-CAFO animal agriculture causes animals to suffer, as well as upon whether the use and killing involved in animal agriculture is ethically problematic even if suffering is minimized.
- *Does the argument extend to all products resulting from animal agriculture, such as dairy and eggs?* Whether the argument should be extended in this way depends upon whether the production of animal products other than meat involves causing unjustified suffering (which may vary among forms of animal agriculture), as well as upon whether the use of animals for our ends is itself ethically problematic.

- *Does the argument extend to aquatic animals, with regard to both wild capture and aquaculture?* Whether the argument should be extended to aquatic animals depends upon whether they have the capacity to suffer, as well as upon whether the practices involved cause them (or others) to suffer. As discussed earlier, feeling pain is not merely a matter of responding to stimuli (which plants do) or having bare sensations, but requires experiencing things as unpleasant or undesirable. This will likely differ among aquatic animals. It may be that cephalopods (e.g. octopi) and fish suffer, whereas clams and oysters do not. This extension also depends upon whether the use and killing of animals for our purposes is itself ethically problematic. (The ethics of commercial fishing is discussed at greater length later on in this chapter.)

- *Would the argument apply if agricultural animals could be created that are less sensitive to pain or not sentient—e.g. engineered so that they lack the necessary brain structures or have diminished nerve sensitivity?* There have been several research projects along these lines, with very limited success. Whether the argument would apply to insentient (or much less sensitive) animals depends upon whether the animals would be due similar consideration to non-diminished animals (or if their moral status would be more like that of plants), upon whether the interests of an animal include not being killed (in addition to not suffering), and upon whether an animal rights view on the moral considerability of animals is more justified than an animal welfare view. A related animal welfare issue is whether it is problematic to try to create diminished animals, due to the suffering and death likely to be involved in the development process.

- *What constitutes a sufficiently good reason to eat meat produced in ways that cause animals to suffer?* This dimension concerns the circumstances of consumption to which the argument extends. According to the claims in support of the argument, basic and serious interests, such as life and health, are adequately justifying, whereas mere preferences for taste are not. But what about the areas in between, such as situations and practices connected with heritage, culture, community and religion? (The ethical significance of cultural practice is discussed at length in Chapter 6.)

ARGUMENT FROM ECOLOGICAL IMPACTS

Many people are opposed to animal agriculture and eat a non-meat diet for ecological reasons. Here is the core ecological argument against eating meat:

1. We ought to act in ways that reduce the ecological impacts of our diet.
2. Adopting a non-meat diet would significantly reduce the ecological impacts of our diet.
3. Therefore, we ought to adopt a non-meat diet.

Premise one—we ought to act in ways that reduce the ecological impacts of our diet—is taken to be justified by the enormous environmental impacts of intensive agriculture. With respect to land use, approximately 38% of the terrestrial surface of the earth is used for agriculture, and deforestation for agriculture, particularly in tropical regions, occurred at a rate of 13 million hectares/year (an area approximately the size of Costa Rica) from 2000 to 2010 (FAO, 2010). Agriculture often depletes natural resources more quickly than they can be replenished. In the United States, 80% of freshwater usage is agricultural, and worldwide 70% of freshwater usage is agricultural. Conventional agriculture involves introducing large amounts of chemicals into the environment. In the United States alone, approximately 900 million pounds of pesticides and herbicides are used in agriculture each year, along with more than 12 million tons of nitrogen fertilizer (USDA, 2013a). Agriculture, forestry and other land uses (AFOLU) are responsible for approximately 24% of greenhouse gas emissions (IPCC, 2014; FAO, 2014a). Approximately half of these emissions are directly from agriculture, and nearly two thirds of agricultural emissions are associated with livestock. The majority of the remaining emissions from the AFOLU sectors are from deforestation, which is largely done for agricultural purposes (FAO, 2014a; FAOSTAT, 2014b). Animal agriculture also generates very large amounts of waste. Dairy cattle, for example, produce twenty to forty times more waste per day than adult humans. In the United States, the agricultural excrement produced each year contains more than 2 million tons of phosphorus and 6 million tons of nitrogen. Livestock, particularly in high concentrations, can also cause erosion, soil compaction and devegetation (EPA, 2014b; MacDonald and McBride, 2009).

The ecological impacts of intensive agriculture are detrimental for people, animals, ecosystems, and even agricultural systems. Habitat destruction remains the leading cause of biodiversity loss. Agricultural chemicals and animal waste pollute the air and water that people, communities, and nonhuman species depend upon. Global climate change involves changes in precipitation patterns, surface air temperatures, sea levels and extreme weather events that are detrimental to agricultural productivity, create environmental refugees, and increase extinction rates (IPCC, 2014). The impacts of anthropogenic climate change are expected to grow dramatically in the coming decades. On some mid and upper level greenhouse gas emissions scenarios, over a third of plant and animal species could be committed to extinction by the middle of this century (Thomas et al., 2004; IPCC, 2007) and there could be hundreds of millions of environmental refugees, resulting in mass migrations and violent conflicts (DSB, 2011). Whereas the argument from animal welfare depends upon the moral considerability of animals, the ecological argument can appeal to the moral considerability of people, animals and/or ecological systems, since agriculture's ecological impacts are detrimental to the health and well-being of each of these.

Premise two—adopting a non-meat diet would significantly reduce the ecological impacts of our diet—is based on two considerations. The first is that many of the detrimental impacts of agriculture are associated with the animals themselves—e.g. their waste and their emissions. The second is that producing calories from animals is enormously inefficient. This was discussed at length in the previous chapter. Because ten calories fed to cattle results in only one calorie consumed by people, ten times more crop agriculture is needed to get the same amount of calories from beef than if the crops are directly consumed. This means ten times as much ecological impact—ten times more land, ten times more water, ten times more fuel, ten times more chemical inputs, ten times more soil depletion—just for the crop agriculture involved. Then there are the additional water, fuel and chemicals used in the animal agriculture itself. The inefficiencies are not as large with respect to fowl and swine, but they are nevertheless highly ecologically significant. (As mentioned in the previous chapter, insect rearing is much more efficient than raising livestock.)

If we have strong ethical reasons, grounded in human, animal and ecosystem health and welfare, to reduce the ecological impacts of our diets (premise 1), and foregoing eating meat would dramatically reduce our diets' impacts (premise 2), then we have strong ethical reasons to adopt a non-meat diet.

OBJECTIONS TO THE ARGUMENT FROM ECOLOGICAL IMPACTS

The objections to the argument from ecological impacts echo many of those to the argument from animal welfare. For instance, it is often pointed out that the ecological impacts of all forms of animal agriculture are not equal. The argument focuses on the unintended impacts, inefficient resource utilization, and externalization of ecological costs associated with intensive animal agriculture or CAFOs. However, there are more sustainable and efficient forms of animal agriculture, in which animals are ranged or rotated through agricultural fields to eat weedy plants and fertilize the soil, for example. There are also sources of meat—e.g. hunting and animals killed on roadways—which are not agricultural and in many cases do not have negative ecological impacts associated with them. Therefore, the argument should not be applied to all meat eating, but only to eating meat produced through ecologically detrimental practices. It is also often contended that the argument must be sensitive to circumstances. If people need to eat animals for health reasons, because they do not have adequate access to alternatives, or as an important component of cultural practice, then there should be an exception. The challenge of inconsequentialism applies as well, since unilaterally forgoing meat is not going to materially reduce the ecological impacts of animal agriculture.

The responses to these objections are the same as those raised regarding the argument from animal welfare. They are presented above, so do not need repeating here. (See "Limited scope," "Meat eating is not a mere preference," and "Appeal to inconsequentialism.")

However, there is one prominent objection to the argument from ecological impacts that does not have an analog in the argument from animal welfare discourse. The argument from ecological impacts assumes that if people significantly reduce the amount of meat that they consume, there will be a decrease in crop agriculture because we will produce much less grain for animal feed. However, this may not be the case. It might be that crop production levels are maintained, but that a much larger share goes to non-food purposes, such as biofuels, and/or that a larger food supply not diverted to meat production will mean lower food prices and so greater food access and consumption for those who are currently food insecure.

In response, proponents of the argument acknowledge that there will not be a perfect relationship between reduced meat consumption and reduced crop agriculture. However, in places where the majority of the grain crop is used for animal feed (e.g. the United States), it is unlikely that biofuels will be able to pick up the excess created with a shift away from animal agriculture. This is particularly so as next generation cellulose-based and algal-based biofuels are developed, which will not require food crops as inputs. Moreover, even if crop production remains high, the ecological impacts associated with the animals themselves would be eliminated— e.g. methane emissions and waste. Furthermore, if the outcome of reduced CAFO meat consumption would be improved food access for the global poor, then that is a strong argument for reducing meat consumption. In fact, it is a key premise in the *argument from distributive justice* discussed below.

As with the argument from animal welfare, the argument from ecological impacts is strongest when focused on routinely eating meat produced from CAFOs, and one of the core questions about the argument is how far beyond that it extends. For example, is it applicable to other forms of animal agriculture (e.g. are the ecological impacts of ranching—such as soil compaction and erosion around water sources, predator eliminations, and changes to vegetation patterns—sufficient for the argument to apply?)? Does it imply that we should forgo all animal products? Are cultural and religious considerations sufficiently important to justify meat consumption? Does it extend to aquaculture and wild fish capture, and if so, which forms and types? (For example, as discussed in Chapter 1, shrimp aquaculture has very large ecological impacts, and salmon aquaculture, like CAFO production, is highly inefficient, whereas tilapia aquaculture is less so (Costa-Pierce et al., 2011).) The primary difference between the two arguments at the value and principle level is that the argument from animal welfare depends upon the moral considerability of animals, whereas the argument from ecological impacts can appeal to the worth of people, animals, and/or ecological systems and biodiversity.

ARGUMENT FROM DISTRIBUTIVE JUSTICE

Another prominent argument for refraining from eating meat—particularly meat from CAFOs—is the argument from distributive justice. Like the ecological argument, this argument trades on the inefficiencies of meat production. As has been discussed above, meat production provides a negative nutritional return on investment—you must put more calories and nutrition into the animals than you get out of them. Therefore, if people were to significantly reduce the amount of meat in their diets, there would be more calories available to the food system. An expanded food supply should result in reduced food prices and increased food access for many of the 842 million people who are malnourished.

The operative ethical principle in this argument concerns the distribution or allocation of scarce resources: *if you are using more resources than you need, and others are suffering for lack of those resources, then you ought to forgo some of your resources to make more available to them.* The considerations typically offered in support of this principle are those appealed to in order to justify a responsibility of assistance: compassion, historical and structural injustices, moral luck, and the equal worth of people. In fact, the principle is really an alternative, more formal, formulation of the principle of assistance discussed in the previous chapter: *a person should give so long as it does not significantly impact her own welfare.* If we have a responsibility to use some of our resources—as individuals or nations—to reduce global food insecurity, then significantly reducing our inefficient meat consumption is one way to fulfill that responsibility. Moreover, because reduced CAFO meat production would be positive in terms of ecological impacts and animal welfare, this approach to promoting food access has significant ancillary benefits.

The soundness of this argument depends upon whether the principle of distributive justice that it appeals to is justified. This principle, and the ethical considerations on which it is based, were discussed at length in Chapter 2 and do not need repeating here. (See the sections entitled "National obligations" and "Individual obligations.") The argument's soundness also depends upon whether reducing meat consumption would in fact reduce malnutrition. As discussed in the previous section, this hinges upon what the impacts of reduced meat consumption would be on agricultural production and food distribution. There is a bit of tension between the distributive justice argument and the ecological argument for reducing CAFO-produced meat consumption. The ecological argument depends upon reductions in crop (and animal) agriculture, while the distributive justice argument depends upon crop calories still being produced and getting to those in need. Either way, however, there is an argument for reduced meat consumption.

ARGUMENT FROM HEALTH

An argument sometimes made in support of not eating animals is *the argument from health*, which posits that a non-meat diet is healthier than a meat-based diet. On this view, there are prudential reasons in favor of reducing meat consumption, as well as a responsibility to not feed large amounts of meat to your children. As with most arguments in applied ethics (including those already discussed in this chapter), there are two aspects to this argument that need to be considered, the normative principle and the empirical claims. Is it true that a non-meat diet is healthier than a meat-based diet? Is it true that, if it is healthier, this grounds a responsibility to not eat meat?

It certainly is possible to eat a healthy diet without eating meat. There are hundreds of millions of examples of this. It is also clearly possible to eat a healthy diet containing meat. There are hundreds of millions of examples of this. Moreover, as will be discussed in Chapter 5, there are food safety challenges with meat, fresh vegetables, seafood, dairy and virtually every other type of food. For most people in countries with food abundance, the injunction to "eat healthy" can be readily satisfied with either a diet containing some meat or a diet containing no meat. Health considerations might justify eating less meat than is typically done in some places, such as the United States, or avoiding meat that is prepared in certain ways or has come from certain types of sources. However, good health and prudence do not appear to require giving up meat altogether.

Moreover, even if a diet containing meat was less healthy than a non-meat diet, it is unlikely that this would ground a moral or ethical responsibility to give it up. After all, there are many things that people do that have risks associated with them—e.g. downhill skiing and drinking alcohol. These are not unethical, even though they are unnecessary and serve only peripheral interests. It is imprudent to ski without a helmet, and it is irresponsible to have your children do so. Similarly, it is imprudent to eat undercooked meat, and it is irresponsible to have your children do so. However, meat eating as such, even if it is statistically less healthy in the long run than a non-meat diet, is not so dangerous or so detrimental when done properly that there is an ethical or moral responsibility to avoid it.

ARGUMENT FROM THE SEXUAL POLITICS OF MEAT

The argument from the sexual politics of meat, most famously developed by Carol Adams, is based on the connection between gender, power and meat in many societies. The argument has two key components. The first is that there is a problematic power relationship between men and women in Western (and many non-Western) cultures, in which men are empowered over women. The second is that there is a cultural connection between conceptions of manliness and meat eating that expresses, embodies and helps to perpetuate the problematic power relationships and associated cultural practices.

The history of Western thought, both religious and philosophical, is filled with dichotomous thinking in which the world is divided into two categories and one is set as superior to the other: human vs. nature, reason vs. emotion, and male vs. female. Not only is there a value orientation of human/reason/male over nature/emotion/female, but the former has historically been enjoined to control the latter. One of the functions of reason is to moderate our passions and urges. Nature and animals are resources to be subdued and used by people as needed. Men are heads of the household, and women are to submit to them. Only men are able to serve as religious or political leaders, permitted to own land, or have the right to vote. Women are treated as property (like animals), the rights over which can be given, sold or exchanged.

While we might be inclined to think that so problematic a patriarchal culture is a thing of the past, a frank look at contemporary cultural practices reveals that this is not the case. For one thing, many of the historical examples cited above persist. In many religions, women are excluded from high leadership still today. In many places in the world, women cannot hold property, and they still can be given or purchased (or, more precisely, access to the sexual use of their bodies can be given or purchased). Women are also not permitted to participate in governance or civic life in many places, are required to wear (or prohibited from wearing) particular clothing, are not permitted to drive, cannot reveal their skin (or hair) or go into public spaces unattended, and are excluded from certain educations or professions. These are all ways in which women are disempowered: they are treated in ways that limit their autonomy and maintain male control and dominance over them.

Even in nations in which there are no longer legal exclusions and restrictions, the problematic power relationships persist. Men are still widely regarded as head-of-household decision-makers, whereas women are regarded as more emotional and nurturing, and they are disproportionately responsible for maintaining the home and raising children (even when they are in the workforce). Women are underrepresented in leadership positions in governance, business and high-status, high-earning professions, and dramatically overrepresented in lower-paying, lower-status, caregiving professions such as social work and childcare. For example, women hold only 18.5% of the seats in the U.S. Congress, while in the UK only 23% of Parliament consists of women; in Turkey, the figure is 14% (World Bank, 2014b). Only 4.6% of Fortune 500 and Fortune 1,000 companies have a woman as their CEO (Catalyst, 2014). Only 25% of the IT workforce in the United States consists of women, while women make up over 90% of the paid childcare workforce (Department of Labor, 2014). Sexism and sexual harassment are also common in the workplace. In a recent study in the UK, a third of women reported experiencing gender-related barriers to advancement during their careers (Robert Half, 2014), and in the United States there were over 27,000 sex-based discrimination charges and over 7,000 sexual harassment charges filed (82.4% by women) in 2013 (EEOC, 2014a; EEOC, 2014b). There are lingering perceptions that girls are less capable at the "rational" subjects of math, computers and science than are boys. Being called "girly" is an insult to a boy because it is meant to call out lack of strength, confidence and power. Moreover, women are routinely objectified. This occurs through everything from beauty pageants, to music videos, to advertisements, to pornography. The message presented to girls by Western popular culture is that the most important thing is how they look and that they are attractive, not whether they excel at academics, athletics or creativity. Misogyny is rampant, and it is casually accepted and encouraged in popular culture, including sports, video games, advertising, music, fashion and reality television. That patriarchy, sexism, gender discrimination, problematic gender roles and ideals, and misogyny persist and are perpetuated in these and other ways is the first component of the argument from the sexual politics of meat.

The second component of the argument is the role that food, and meat in particular, plays in this cultural context. Sexism, sexual discrimination, sexual harassment and sexual assault occur throughout the food industry (as they do everywhere) in agricultural fields, fast food chains, agro-food corporations, food publications, and high-end restaurants. Domestic food preparation is disproportionately the responsibility of women. Food consumption is connected to culturally idealized feminine bodies, particularly thinness. These ideals are not connected to good health, but rather to conceptions of beauty and sexuality. They foster high levels of food monitoring, dieting and eating disorders, such as bulimia and anorexia, while men are encouraged to eat heartily and to build strength. Women are routinely objectified, badly treated, and cast as food preparers in food and beverage advertisements. Foods are themselves gendered. Everyone knows who eats yogurt and salad, and who eats meat and potatoes; who drinks wine spritzers and who drinks beer. Meat consumption is connected to masculinity, strength and power, and it expresses problematically gendered ideals, roles, expectations, stereotypes and relationships. Real men kill and eat meat; and real women prepare it for them and watch them eat it. The argument from the sexual politics of meat concludes that we ought to reject eating meat as part of the rejection of a patriarchal culture in which men and masculinity are valorized and set over women and femininity, and in which women (like animals and nature) are objectified and treated as mere things to be used, consumed and "hunted" as trophies and conquests by men. Women, particularly when objectified or demeaned, are often referred to by animal terms—"vixens," "birds," "chicks" and "bitches." They are dehumanized. Similarly, animals are de-individualized and even de-animalized (and so made invisible) when they are for human use—"broilers," "layers," "livestock" and "game." To consume meat in this context is to be implicated in the cultural problems and associations surrounding and permeating it.

Responses to the argument from the sexual politics of meat typically do not challenge the claim that many, if not most, cultures remain problematically patriarchal in the ways discussed above. Nor do they challenge the facts that women are routinely objectified, that sexism and gender discrimination remain commonplace, that sexual harassment and assault are widespread, and that problematic gender roles, expectations, stereotypes and ideals are the norm. The evidence is simply too strong. (They will sometimes point out that there are problematic ideals, stereotypes and expectations for men and masculinity as well.) Responses also do not challenge the claim that meat eating historically has been and remains gendered. (They do argue that this is much less so today than in the past and that meat eating is typically not consciously conceived of in this way.) Instead, challenges to the argument often take the form of contending that giving up meat consumption is not the only or even the best way to reject patriarchal culture and the objectification of women, animals (particularly livestock) and nature. The alternative is to co-opt meat eating and to take this symbol of patriarchy and use it as a source of empowerment and strength. Women should eat heartily. They should eat healthfully. They should eat meat. We should reject the genderedness of food, not by conceding meat, but by empowering women to be consumers and not only preparers of it.

In reply to this response, proponents of the argument sometimes emphasize that there are really two types of gendered problems with meat eating. The first is the way in which meat is implicated to problematic gender roles, relationships and expectations. The second is the connection between the objectification of women and the objectification of nature and animals. The response given above addresses the first of these, but not the second, since it would continue treating animals as mere things to be mass produced for our consumption (particularly when they are from CAFOs).

AN OBLIGATION TO EAT MEAT (AND HUNT)?

It is sometimes argued that, far from being impermissible, there is actually an obligation to eat meat. One common type of argument for this conclusion involves appeals to historical and biological facts about us. For example, humans are physiologically capable of eating meat, we evolved the capacity to eat meat because it was advantageous for our ancestors to do so, and we have always eaten meat in the past. These types of arguments commit the *fallacy of appeal to nature* and the *fallacy of appeal to tradition*. The fact that people are capable of doing something does not imply that it is permissible for them to do it. Human history has shown that we are capable of a great many horrors, such as genocide, slavery and torture. Moreover, the fact that something was advantageous in the past (or even the present) in terms of increasing biological fitness does not tell us that we ought to do it. Fitness (in evolutionary theory) is a biological concept that figures into explanations of how traits arise, not a moral or ethical one that justifies actions or behaviors. If killing competitors and forcing copulation were fitness-enhancing, it would still be unethical. Furthermore, just because people have done something in the past does not mean it is obligatory or even permissible to do it in the future—after all, there is a long human history of waging war for economic gain and restricting the rights and autonomy of women. (The ethical significance of cultural traditions and practices is discussed at length in Chapter 6.)

Another type of argument for an obligation to eat meat appeals to ecological facts about the world. For example, other predators eat meat—lions eat gazelles—so it is permissible and perhaps a biological imperative that we do so as well. Moreover, we have an obligation to hunt in order to prevent prey species from becoming overpopulated, particularly when their natural predators have been eliminated (by us). The first of these arguments, like those discussed above, commits the fallacy of appeal to nature. Nature is not an ethical guide for us—lions keep prides and sometimes kill their young, as well. The second argument is more promising. As discussed earlier in this chapter ("Argument from ecological impacts"), it appears that we do have a responsibility to help promote the integrity and stability of ecological systems, and this may involve preventing overpopulation of some species. However, it does not immediately follow from this that we should hunt and kill them. Perhaps we should, instead, reintroduce the predators that were eliminated, or find non-lethal means of population management. Moreover, even if the argument is sound, it is not an argument for an obligation to eat meat. It is an argument for an obligation to, in some cases, use lethal means to control some populations of some species (and then perhaps to eat them in some cases so as not to be wasteful).

A third type of argument for eating meat appeals to animal welfare. According to the *conscientious carnivore argument*, the best way to end problematic CAFO practices is for people to eat meat and insist upon humanely raised animals. Refraining from eating meat does not provide an incentive for producers to treat their animals well, whereas expanding the market for compassionately produced meat does. This argument is meant to complement the animal welfare and ecological arguments discussed above. It takes those arguments as being successful in showing that CAFOs are ethically unacceptable and then adds the claim that eating meat from alternative sources is a more effective way to undermine them than is rejecting meat eating altogether. This is an empirical claim, and I do not know of any data that either supports it or challenges it. However, as a market-based argument, the key is to reduce demand for CAFO meat, and this would seem to be equally accomplished by rejecting CAFO meat along with all other meat or by rejecting CAFO meat while eating meat that is humanely produced. In response, proponents of this argument might emphasize that conscientious carnivorism, unlike refraining from meat eating altogether, both undermines CAFOs and supports local, humane meat production. In so doing, it helps to provide an alternative to CAFOs that may appeal to those who are not willing to give up meat altogether.

ETHICAL DIMENSIONS OF HUNTING

Agriculture is not the only way to procure food. It is also possible to forage, fish and hunt. All hunting involves intentionally killing animals. However, there are many different reasons, not mutually exclusive, why people engage in hunting:

- *Subsistence*—Hunting is sometimes done in order to meet basic nutritional needs. Examples of subsistence hunting include bush meat hunting in parts of central Africa and caribou hunting by the Inupiat in parts of the Arctic. In these cases, hunting provides a crucial source of protein.

- *Cultural*—Hunting is sometimes done as part of cultural traditions or practices. Cultural hunting includes traditional hunting by indigenous peoples, such as the Makah who hunt grey whales on the Pacific Northwestern coast of the United States, as well as Inupiat caribou hunting just mentioned. It also includes hunting by non-indigenous peoples when it is viewed by them as part of their cultural identities—e.g. ungulate, fowl and bear hunting in many parts of the United States.

- *Sport*—Hunting is sometimes done as a recreational activity. This includes large game trophy hunting, hunting competitions, and hunting for fun generally.

- *Ecological management*—There are many reasons why hunting occurs as part of ecosystem management programs. It is done to reduce populations that are regarded as overpopulated and ecologically detrimental, such as white-tailed deer in many parts of the United States. It is done to help to prevent the spread of animals beyond designated areas, as is done with Yellowstone bison that move beyond the boundaries of the park and adjacent protected areas. It is very often done to eliminate non-native species (e.g. ruddy ducks in the UK and rabbits in Australia) and feral populations (e.g. goats and pigs in the Galapagos Islands and the Channel Islands off California).

- *Economic*—Hunting/harvesting is often done for trade, to protect agriculture, or out of other economic interests. Examples of economic hunting include harp seal pup hunts in Norway, Canada, Greenland and Namibia; poaching elephants for ivory and bush meat for sale in Africa; and selling hunting licenses for everything from wolves to moose to grouse in the United States.

- *Public safety*—Hunting is sometimes done to protect the public or to eliminate nuisances. Examples of this include hunting particular animals that pose threats to people (or their livelihood), such as bear, big cats or elephants that have become aggressive and attracted to human activities, as well as reducing populations to decrease car accidents and disease transmission (as with white-tailed deer in the United States). It also includes controlling bothersome populations, as is sometimes done with crows and pigeons in urban areas.

Some hunting is widely regarded as problematic. For example, the systematic hunting of elephants for ivory by organized groups is illegal and having a devastating impact on their populations. Commercial baby harp seal hunting done to satisfy people's peripheral fashion interests is viewed as cruel (it involves bludgeoning pups in the head) and unnecessary from an ecological and management standpoint. Hunting endangered animals for the medicinal trade—e.g. gorillas and tigers—is among the primary threats to their continued existence in the wild. Canned hunts conducted within enclosed areas and culling contests in which people compete to see how many animals they can kill are seen as unsporting, unskilled, and contrary to hunting ideals involving fair chase. Hunting wolves in Alaska (including by helicopter) to generate license revenue and increase the availability of moose and elk is regarded as wanton and ecologically problematic.

None of the examples in the previous paragraph involve hunting primarily for food (except to the extent that the revenue from economic hunting enables purchasing food). If hunting is crucial to survival and well-being, for subsistence, then it is widely regarded as being ethically acceptable, since it serves basic and serious interests. The more contested and interesting cases are cultural and sport hunting for food (i.e. the killed animal is eaten), when other food sources are available. Thus, the question to be addressed here is whether, and under what conditions, these forms of hunting are ethically acceptable.

There are several types of considerations relevant to the ethical analysis of a hunt, in addition to the reason for hunting. The moral status of the target animals matters. As discussed earlier ("Argument from animal welfare" and "Animal suffering is not morally significant"), moral status is tied to the cognitive and psychological capacities that an entity has (e.g. whether it is sentient), and different animals may have different moral status due to variation in these respects. Moral status can also differ based on relational properties, such as whether a species has protected status or special cultural importance. The location of the hunt can also be ethically significant—e.g. whether it is on private or publicly held lands, or whether it is an open or canned hunt. Hunting methods are also relevant, since different methods—e.g. trap, bow, gun and dog—cause different types of injuries, are differently effective, differentially impact nontarget species, and require different skill sets. For example, trapping is more indiscriminate than bow or gun hunting. The ecological impacts of hunting are also differential. Populations of some species are so large as to be detrimental to the ecological systems of which they are a part—e.g. rabbits in Australia and white-tailed deer in the United States. Other populations, while not over carrying capacity, are robust enough that some hunting can be done without destabilizing them—e.g. black bear and mourning doves in parts of the United States. Still other populations are already significantly reduced, threatened or endangered—e.g. wolves in the continental United States and tigers in India. Finally, hunting ethos is ethically relevant—i.e. how the hunt is conducted and the values or character of those conducting it. It is here that conceptions of sportingness and responsibility come into play, as well as the participant's attitudes and motivations regarding the hunt—e.g. whether they are focused on the experience, the skills involved, or the killing.

It is crucial to take all of these factors into account when evaluating a particular hunt. Hunting using steel jaw traps on public lands where there are threatened species that might unintentionally be killed has a much different ethical profile than does gun hunting white-tailed deer on privately held lands where they are overpopulated to the point that they are detrimental to other species in the ecosystem.

CORE ARGUMENT AGAINST (NON-SUBSISTENCE) HUNTING

The previous section highlighted the different ethical profiles that hunting can have. However, there is one thing that all hunts have in common: they involve the goal of killing an animal. The *core argument against non-subsistence hunting* runs as follows:

1. Recreational and cultural hunting involve the intentional killing of an animal for human purposes.
2. Intentionally killing animals for human purposes is wrong, except to satisfy a basic interest (e.g. self-defense or subsistence).

3. Recreational and cultural hunting is not necessary to satisfy a basic interest.

4. Therefore, recreational and cultural hunting are wrong.

The first premise of this argument is thought to follow from the concept or definition of hunting. As discussed above, killing an animal is not always, or even usually, the primary or only goal of a hunt; and a hunt does not always end with a kill. However, if an activity does not involve the possibility of a kill, if it is not connected to that end at all, then it is difficult to see how it could be considered a hunt.

The second premise, the ethical principle, might be justified by appeal to the worth of the animal hunted and/or the character of the hunter. If animals are morally considerable such that it is wrong to treat them as a mere means for human ends or to not take their interests into consideration, then killing them unnecessarily seems problematic. It may also be that people who are comfortable with such non-necessary killing, who embrace it recreationally or as part of their cultural identity, have a problematic or vicious character. The basis for this claim could be that they are not adequately sensitive to the moral considerability of the target animals, or it could be that their comfort with killing and causing animals to suffer could make them more likely to treat other people badly. The latter is sometimes called an *indirect duties view*. On such views, we have a responsibility to treat animals in certain ways—in this case to refrain from killing them—as an extension of our responsibilities to people.

The third premise of the argument is a substantive claim about the importance of recreational and cultural activities in people's lives. The claim is not that these are unimportant, but that they are not important enough to justify considering them a basic interest. Even if culturally meaningful activities and recreation are crucial to individual well-being, they are not crucial for survival, and they could be met in other, nonlethal ways.

IN DEFENSE OF RECREATIONAL FOOD HUNTING

A common response to the core argument against hunting is to challenge premise two—that intentionally killing animals for human purposes is wrong unless it satisfies a basic interest. One way to do this is by appeal to cases. For example, if we allow killing animals for medical research aimed at non-terminal diseases, then it seems that we must accept killing animals for serious (but not basic) reasons, and perhaps cultural hunting rises to that level of importance. Another response is to challenge the claim that animals are directly morally considerable. This issue was discussed at length above ("Animal suffering is not morally significant"). A third response is to argue that hunting does not necessarily involve insensitivity to the suffering of animals or the worth of animals (even assuming they have it), and that it can express and promote virtue. Ethically responsible hunting aims at killing cleanly and with minimum suffering, for example. It also requires taking responsibility for the killing involved in food production, whereas other forms of production hide the killing and costs involved so that consumers do not need to face up to them.

The idea of taking responsibility for one's food ties into a broader argument in defense of recreational food hunting. Meat from hunting is not necessary to satisfy our basic interests, but food is needed. So the focus of evaluation should be on how hunting compares to other food sources. Proponents of hunting argue that it compares quite favorably from an ethical perspective. One reason for this is that all food production—crop, animal agricultural, commercial fishing, and hunting—involves killing animals. This is clear in the cases of hunting, fishing and animal agriculture. However, crop agriculture (organic and conventional) causes animals to die from habitat loss, chemical inputs, and the use of heavy machinery for tilling, planting and harvesting, which kills large numbers of reptiles, rodents, birds and other field species. It is not possible to eliminate nonhuman death from our food supply, so hunting is not uniquely ethically problematic for involving killing. Furthermore, its proponents argue, hunting has several features that provide it with a positive ethical profile in comparison to agriculture, particularly industrial agriculture:

- *Hunters take responsibility for the source of their food.* Hunters face up to the death involved in acquiring food. They must reconcile with the fact that their food comes with a loss and that it is a taking from others; and they make themselves the agent of this. This is not the case with many other food sources, where the costs and production processes are concealed from consumers. This hiddenness involves not only the absence of agency, but in many cases the absence of awareness. As discussed earlier (Chapter 1), this enables the perpetuation of ethically problematic practices in food systems.

- *Hunted animals have a better quality of life than do livestock.* The lives of animals in industrial agricultural systems are short, full of suffering, and do not allow for species-typical behavior. In contrast, hunted animals live species-typical lives. Their lives are not easy or pleasant—they must avoid predators and compete for resources— but they are the lives of deer, bears, birds, pigs, hares, and so on. Moreover, most hunting codes of ethics emphasize the principle of "fair chase," in which prey have a reasonable chance of escaping and in which success requires skill, patience and knowledge.

- *Hunting does not cause much suffering when done properly.* Most hunting codes of ethics call for hunting only animals that you are skilled enough to take cleanly, taking only kill shots, and quickly tracking and putting down injured animals. Death by hunting can be much quicker and less traumatic than death from deprivation, exposure, predation, or the forms of slaughter used in CAFOs.

- *Hunting does not have the negative ecological impacts of agriculture and can be ecologically beneficial.* The ecological impacts of agriculture—both crop and animal—were discussed at length earlier ("Argument from ecological impacts"). When done properly, and in accordance with hunting codes of ethics, hunting has minimal ecological and habitat impacts. It involves "leave no trace" camping and using vehicles only on designated roadways, for example. Moreover, hunting can be ecologically beneficial when it reduces an ecologically problematic population. It also can be the basis for building ecological knowledge and concern. Principles of good hunting involve learning about prey species, their habitats, and their behaviors. Hunting itself often involves engaging in prolonged periods of listening, watching and moving through ecological systems, thereby building understanding and attentiveness. In North America, many local and national environmental organizations are "hook-and-bullet" in that they are constituted by hunters and anglers concerned about habitat loss, water and air pollution, road building, and sustainable management. In addition, fees from hunting and fishing licenses are often used to fund conservation programs and management activities.

- *Hunting involves killing only animals that are used.* All agriculture involves killing animals. However, hunting codes of ethics emphasize taking only target species, not taking more than one can use, even if it is less than the legal limit, and utilizing as much of the animals as possible. Moreover, when large animals are hunted, a single kill can provide over a hundred pounds of meat. In contrast, the animals killed through crop agriculture are byproducts—e.g. field animals and animals killed by habitat destruction—and are not used. In addition, as discussed in Chapter 2, a large amount of the food that is produced from crop and animal agriculture is lost to spoilage and wastage.
- *Hunting can be socially and culturally significant.* Killing cannot be eliminated from food production. However, with hunting it can be in a form that is socially and culturally significant. It can involve tradition, passing on knowledge, building cultural connections, and strengthening relationships. In agriculture, the killing is often industrial (CAFOs) or incidental (crop agriculture).
- *Hunting has economic benefits.* Hunting and fishing do not have nearly the same economic significance as agriculture. However, in some places the economic activity around hunting can be important. It is the cornerstone of the tourism industry in many remote areas, for example. In the United States in 2011, approximately $73 billion USD was spent on hunting and fishing (USFWS, 2012).
- *Hunting can develop skills, knowledge and character.* Several of the benefits of hunting discussed above involve improving oneself. Being a good, responsible hunter involves a range of skills such as shooting, tracking and concentration. It requires engagement with and knowledge of the natural world. It takes patience, attentiveness, fortitude, responsibility, appreciation and restraint, among other virtues. Learning and engaging in hunting (and fishing) in responsible ways can make a person better—physically, intellectually and morally.

Taken together, these considerations constitute a robust defense of the ethical acceptability of some forms of hunting, in some contexts, done in some ways. As discussed earlier, other forms of hunting do cause a lot of suffering (e.g. trapping), are not ecologically sensitive (e.g. wolf hunting), are not sporting (e.g. canned hunts and culling contests), and are not done responsibly (e.g. with respect to safety, ecological sensitivity, compassion or sportingness). Thus, a conception of what constitutes good or ethical hunting— including acceptable methods, contexts, target species, and attitudes— is embedded in the foregoing defense of hunting. It is not a defense of recreational hunting *as such*.

Moreover, many (though not all) of the goods associated with hunting may be achievable through non-lethal nature activities. Wildlife viewing (e.g. birding) and photography are recreational, require and can help to develop skills, knowledge and character, and are socially and economically significant. In the United States, for example, 29% of the adult population participates in some form of wildlife watching (and they made over $50 billion USD in expenditures on it in 2011), whereas only 6% of the adult population are hunters and 14% anglers (USFWS, 2012). Furthermore, there are alternatives for getting food from nonindustrial sources. Small, local, independent and organic agriculture (including animal agriculture) often have many of the same ecological, animal welfare, and developmental benefits as hunting, when compared with industrial agriculture.

Given the foregoing, perhaps something like the following conclusion is warranted. Recreational and cultural hunting for food can be ethically preferable to eating food produced via conventional industrial agriculture and can be comparable to nonindustrial sources, depending upon such things as ecological impacts, method of hunt, ethos/attitude of hunter, alternatives available, and target species. If this is correct, then hunting for food (even when elective) is not always wrong and should be evaluated on these criteria on a case-by-case basis.

COMMERCIAL FISHING

Aquaculture (farming aquatic species) is largely analogous to animal agriculture. Many of the ethical considerations and arguments that apply to animal agriculture—e.g. ecological impacts, animal welfare, distributive justice, inconsequentialism—apply (in appropriately modified form) to aquatic agriculture. Similarly, subsistence, recreational and cultural fishing are largely analogous to subsistence, recreational and cultural hunting. Again, many of the ethical considerations and arguments that apply to hunting apply (in appropriately modified form) to fishing.

Industrial commercial fishing, on the other hand, does not have a ready analog on land. There is no organized global industry that involves capturing enormous amounts of wild land animals for commercial use. The closest current activity is the bush meat trade, which does involve an enormous amount of animals, but is much more local (bush meat tends to be consumed closer to the point of hunting) and distributed (less centrally organized and coordinated) than is commercial fishing. Moreover, the global bush meat trade, while estimated to generate billions of dollars annually, is largely illegal. In contrast, commercial fishing involves (largely) legal, industrialized and globalized harvesting and trade of wild animals— e.g. fish, shellfish and cephalopods. (In terms of historical analogs, the passenger pigeon and bison industries in North America in the nineteenth century are perhaps the closest land cases.)

As discussed in the previous chapter, approximately 87% of the world's fisheries are fully exploited, overexploited or recovering. This is a truly astounding industrial "accomplishment" given the size of the oceans. Over one in ten people rely on fisheries for their livelihood or well-being (FAO, 2014b). Approximately 900 million tons of fish have been captured each year for the past couple of decades. (Capture has plateaued because fisheries' limits have been reached.) In addition, it is estimated that there is nearly 27 million tons of unintended by-catch each year—i.e. fish and other marine life that are not the commercial target, but that are incidentally caught and killed. (Purse seining, gillnetting, trawling and long-lining are particularly conducive to by-catch.) Large predatory fish have been particularly hard hit, with their populations reduced to 10% of what they had been previously. China has by far the largest commercial fishing industry, with over twice the capture by weight as the EU, which is the next largest (FAO, 2012a). On the current trajectory, it is projected that nearly all major commercial species populations will collapse by 2050 (Worm et al., 2006). This is a major reason why there is enormous pressure to expand aquaculture production—already nearly 50% of commercially available fish is the product of aquaculture (FAO, 2012a)—while also making it more efficient and sustainable. Possibilities for doing so include reducing the use of fishmeal and fishoil as feed, improving pollution management, reducing escape into the wild, and restricting farms from ecologically sensitive locations (e.g. mangrove forests).

ETHICAL CONCERNS ABOUT COMMERCIAL FISHING

One ethical concern about commercial fishing is that it is disrespectful of the moral status of the individual animals that are intentionally and unintentionally caught. Given a capacities-based view on moral considerability, this concern is most salient when members of the target species are cognitively and psychologically complex (in comparison to other animals)—e.g. whales and dolphins. Several organizations are committed to ending the harvest of those species, and there are regulations and international agreements that aim to limit their catch. However, the concern is also raised regarding sharks, rays, sea turtles, cephalopods, and even fish and shellfish more generally. The issue of moral considerability was discussed at length earlier ("Argument from animal welfare" and "Animal suffering is not morally significant"), and does not need repeating here. Suffice it to say, if marine organisms are morally considerable, then that is a relevant ethical consideration when evaluating commercial fishing. However, as the hunting discussion shows, even if marine animals are due ethical consideration, it may still be acceptable to capture them under appropriate conditions and in appropriate ways—e.g. in compassionate, sustainable and targeted ways. Wild fish, like wild deer, have a better or more species-typical life than those that are confined.

Another concern regarding commercial fishing is its ecological impacts. Harvest mortality and by-catch (which includes economic discards, regulatory discards and collateral mortality) constitute a massive, constant biological depletion of aquatic systems. Moreover, because large and predatory fish are particularly hard hit, it reverberates throughout the food web to even non-fished species. In addition to the ecological impacts of the take and by-catch, the fishing process itself is often ecologically destructive. Trawling and dredging—which involve towing nets behind boats—are particularly damaging to the ocean floor and release large plumes of sediment into the water. Commercial fishing impacts, combined with other stressors on aquatic systems, particularly pollution and global climate change, have many people worried about the possible collapse of the ocean ecological systems on which we all depend.

TRAGEDY OF THE COMMONS

Commercial fisheries are a paradigmatic case of a problem called the *tragedy of the commons*. A tragedy of the commons occurs when there is a shared or "common" (or "common-pool") resource that multiple agents have access to and each agent acts in ways that, though individually rationally self-interested, result in the depletion of the resource to everyone's detriment (including their own). Deforestation is a tragedy of the commons; the accumulation of greenhouse gases in the atmosphere is a tragedy of the commons; freshwater depletion is a tragedy of the commons; and overfishing is a tragedy of the commons. They are tragedies of the commons because it is rational for people—in terms of their own economic self-interest, basic needs or quality of life—to clear forest for agricultural land, to hunt for meat, to poach for ivory, to cut down trees for firewood, to pump more water to irrigate fields, to use synthetic fertilizer and pesticide, to catch more fish, or to live a high-emissions consumer lifestyle. However, if everyone does so, the cumulative impact is the degradation or depletion of the resource base on which the activity depends and/or secondary effects that are detrimental to everyone in the long run. It results in biodiversity loss, polluted waterways, pesticide-resistant insects, global climate change, reduced agricultural productivity, landslides, and fisheries collapses. The *commons problem* is how to manage or treat such resources in ways that do not result in their degradation.

Commons problems are solvable. Not all shared or common resources are used in ways that end in tragedies. In fact, several (non-exclusive) types of management strategies are used to forestall overuse. These include: privatization; management by a trustee (or holding the resource in public trust); the use of quotas, licensing and take limits; increasing the cost to use the commons (e.g. through taxation or fee-for-use); prohibiting access; and ethical restraint (e.g. out of obligation to future generations). National parks and forests, private land trusts, emissions permits, pollution regulation, hunting permits (and seasons), carbon taxes, endangered species laws, and fishing licenses and take limits are all attempts to address commons problems, and they are frequently successful.

However, not all commons problems are equally easy to address. Successfully managing commons problems is more difficult the less socially and politically connected the users of a common resource; the less clear it is who has authority or jurisdiction to govern a commons, or the less power the authority has; the less well defined the common resource; the larger the number of agents involved; the less congruence there is between the users of the commons and those who suffer from its overuse; and the less congruence there is between those who shoulder the cost of management and those who gain from successful management. For example, global climate change is frequently described as the ultimate commons problem because it has so many features that are inimical to organizing a solution—globalness, diffuse agents, lack of strong (or clear) authority, and spatial, temporal and social incongruence between those most responsible for creating the problem and those who will be most affected by it.

Some fisheries have features that make them quite easy commons problems to manage. For example, Atlantic lobster fisheries in North America have a target species that does not migrate far, is easy to monitor, and about which quite a lot is known. The fishing communities are relatively small and well defined, and the agents are known to each other. There are clear authorities, resources for enforcement, and established methods of conflict resolution. There is high congruence between those who must shoulder the burden of restraint and those who benefit from it in the long run. However, management of many other marine species, particularly migratory species and populations that do not coincide with political jurisdictions, is much more difficult. The agents are diffuse, under different economic pressures, and fall under different political regimes. There are not easily agreed-upon management goals. There is not a strong, clear authority. The populations are difficult to monitor, and there is limited knowledge of their behavior (e.g. migratory routes and reproductive cycles). Violations of agreements can be difficult to monitor and to enforce.

In the end, it may be possible to solve the commons problem for many fisheries. For example, in the United States 32 stocks (e.g. Coho Salmon and Atlantic Swordfish) have been rebuilt since

2000 (NOAA, 2012). However, the same will not be easy for large migratory species, such as shark and tuna, which cross many political boundaries and international waters. One approach that has been proposed, which would also address many of the ecological impacts of commercial fishing, is to restrict the types of methods that can be used. The highest capture-rate approaches—e.g. trawling, purse seining, and gillnetting—are also those with the highest by-catch rates and ecological impacts.

As alluded to above, global fisheries depletion is not the only commons problem related to agriculture. Some common-pool resources are essential agricultural inputs—e.g. freshwater and range land. Other common-pool resources are impacted by agricultural byproducts—e.g. fertilizer and chemical runoff (water), animal waste (water and air), and greenhouse gas emissions (atmosphere). Thus, developing effective, just and sustainable solutions to commons problems is a crucial component of agricultural ethics.

CONCLUSION

The considerations discussed in this chapter favor the conclusion that meat and fish consumption can have diverse ethical profiles. Agriculture has enormous ecological and animal impacts. We ought to reduce those impacts for a variety of ethical reasons (e.g. human rights, animal welfare, and preservation of biodiversity). It seems clear that a highly effective and scalable way to do this is for people with food abundance to adopt a non-farmed-meat diet (or a low farmed-meat diet), particularly with respect to meat produced through CAFOs. This may also promote food availability. However, compassionate, ecologically sensitive, and responsible meat eating also seems possible. Some forms of animal agriculture, some aquaculture, some hunting, and some fishing can meet these standards. However, in each case, they cannot scale up to nearly the level of meat and fish consumption that occurs in many affluent countries today. To do that, they would have to industrialize in ways that would likely undermine their ethical acceptability. So, if we take the question "Should we eat animals?" as asking "Can eating animals be part of an ethically conscientious diet?," the answer appears to be, "Yes it can, but not in the form or quantity that presently exists in high-meat-consuming nations."

FURTHER READING

Several of the books on food systems and food ethics listed at the end of Chapter 1 address the question of whether we ought to eat animals and, if so, which ones. Some influential and thought-provoking works that focus specifically on the issue of animals include:

Thomas Regan, *The Case for Animal Rights* (University of California Press)
Peter Singer, *Animal Liberation* (HarperCollins)
Rosalind Hursthouse, *Ethics, Humans and Other Animals* (Routledge)
Steve Sapontzis, ed., *Food for Thought: The Debate over Eating Meat* (Prometheus)
Carol Adams, *The Sexual Politics of Meat: A Feminist-Vegetarian Critical Theory* (Bloomsbury)
Jonathan Safron Foer, *Eating Animals* (Back Bay Books)
J.M. Coetzee, *The Lives of Animals* (Princeton University Press)

Some thoughtful books that focus on hunting and angling in particular include:

Jim Posewitz, *Beyond Fair Chase: The Ethic and Tradition of Hunting* (Falcon Publishing)
Ted Kerasote, *Bloodties: Nature, Culture, and the Hunt* (Kodansha)
Charles List, *Hunting, Fishing, and Environmental Virtue* (Oregon State University Press)
J. Claude Evans, *With Respect for Nature: Living as Part of the Natural World* (State University of New York Press)

Two seminal works on common-pool resource problems are:

Elinor Ostrom, *Governing the Commons: The Evolution of Institutions for Collective Action* (Cambridge University Press)
Garrett Hardin, *Living within Limits: Ecology, Economics, and Population Taboos* (Oxford University Press)

4

BIOENGINEERING

All food systems are permeated with technology. We use technology to cultivate, capture, harvest, process, transport, store, monitor, sell, prepare and consume food. Although technology is widely accepted in food production and consumption in general, particular technologies and engineering practices are often contested. Over the last few decades, bioengineering agricultural organisms has been especially controversial. Genetically modified (GM) crops and animals are objected to on health, cultural, aesthetic, ecological and moral grounds. There are currently several state-level ballot initiatives in the United States on mandatory labeling of foods containing GM organisms. Test fields of GM rice were recently destroyed in the Philippines. GM policy in the EU is being challenged by some member nations and through international trade agreements. At the same time, researchers are developing new GM crops, which they argue are crucial to meeting our food challenges, and their proponents are advocating for less burdensome regulatory approval processes, so that their benefits can be fully realized. Researchers also continue to engineer animals in novel ways. Cloned livestock has been approved for human consumption by the United States Food and Drug Administration, and salmon engineered for accelerated growth is currently under regulatory review. There is also increasing interest in synthetic or cultured meat—i.e. growing animal tissue for human consumption in bioreactors rather than "on the hoof." This chapter focuses on the ethical discourse surrounding bioengineering in agriculture, particularly GM crops, GM animals and synthetic meat.

GENETIC ENGINEERING: BACKGROUND AND CONTEXT

People have been intentionally hybridizing organisms from different species for millennia by means of breeding and grafting. This is more frequently done in plants than animals, since it is more readily accomplished with them (due to reproduction rates, processes and fecundity, as well as the costs and care demands involved) and the offspring are often viable and fertile. Wheat, grapefruit, tangelo, peppermint and plumcot are examples of interspecific hybrid food plants. However, there are a large number of intentionally created interspecific hybrid animals as well, such as the mule (donkey-horse) and the beefalo (bison-domesticated cow).

Although immensely successful in producing organisms with desirable and useful traits, hybridization through traditional breeding techniques has significant limitations. For instance, there is a lack of control over which traits offspring receive from each parent (which is why back-breeding is needed), and there are constraints on possible genetic combinations (due to sexual compatibility and viability). Beginning with the development of recombinant DNA techniques in the 1970s, these constraints have been increasingly loosened. The techniques enable isolation of genes that code for particular desired traits in individuals of one species and insertion of those genes into the genome of an individual of another species. This makes possible the creation of organisms that have genomic material from species that could never have reproduced or combined in the absence of intentional gene-level intervention—e.g. goats with golden orb spider genes, rice with maize genes, maize with bacteria genes, and salmon with ocean pout genes. These are *transgenic organisms* in that they contain genes from more than on species. (*Intragenic organisms* are engineered by the insertion of genetic material into an individual of the same species.) In addition to agricultural applications, genetically engineered hybrids have been created for biomedical, scientific, conservation and recreational purposes.

The knowledge base and technology needed for genomic sequencing, isolating genes, determining gene functions, knocking out genes, and assembling genomic material, while still quite imperfect, has progressed to the point where it is possible to intensively engineer genomes using elements from multiple biological and synthetic sources. One research group has engineered a yeast that produces high concentrations of artemisinic acid—the precursor for artemisinin, an antimalarial drug—by transplanting genes from sweet wormwood, the traditional source of artemisinin, and several bacteria species, which code for the requisite metabolic pathway, into the yeast. Industrial production of artemisinin using this engineered yeast is underway. *E. coli* have been intensively genetically engineered so that they can break down cellulose in switchgrass and convert it into fuel (or fuel precursors) for diesel, jet fuel and petrol. Similarly, *C. cellulolyticum* have been engineered to convert cellulose into isobutanol. The trend in genomic design and construction is that the base organism is less and less a constraint on what can be created.

The bioengineering of animals for agricultural purposes is also proceeding apace. As mentioned above, goats have already had golden orb spider genes inserted into their genome, so that they produce protein precursors for silk in their milk. Cloned animals are already being sold on the market and have been cleared for human consumption (because they are so expensive they are almost exclusively purchased for breeding purposes). Salmon have been engineered with ocean pout genes so that they grow more rapidly. Bioengineering is even being explored as a means of aiding depleted fish stocks. For example, it is possible to use non-endangered species of fish as surrogates to produce threatened species. Trout spermatogonia inserted into otherwise sterile male and female salmon have resulted in salmon that have only trout offspring.

The mere existence of interspecific individuals is not out of the ordinary. Cross-species hybridization is common among both plants and animals in the wild due to the vagaries and dynamism of the biological world. Moreover, as discussed above, it has long been employed in agriculture to engineer organisms with advantageous traits. Nevertheless, many people find genetic modification by intentional intervention at the genomic level objectionable, particularly when it involves combining genomic material from species that are not otherwise reproductively compatible. In what follows, I provide an overview of the ethics of the transgenic bioengineering of crops before turning to bioengineered animals.

GENETICALLY MODIFIED CROPS

Hundreds of varieties of GM crops have been created. However, only a small number of those are commercially cultivated. The most common GM crops are corn, cotton, soybeans, beets and canola that have been engineered with bacteria genes to be resistant to general-use herbicides, particularly Monsanto's Roundup herbicide (Roundup Ready) and Bayer's Liberty herbicide (LibertyLink). These same commodity crops have also been engineered to produce their own pesticide. These are called Bt crops, since the gene that confers the trait is from a bacterium called *Bacillus thuringiensis*. Crops engineered to be disease-resistant are also currently cultivated. The most prominent of these is papaya engineered to be resistant to a mosaic virus that had previously threatened yields in Hawaii; some virus-resistant squash is also cultivated, and GM cassava resistant to a virus that has decimated yields in parts of Africa has been in development for some time.

The first-generation GM crops described above are engineered primarily for traits that are advantageous to growers. Herbicide resistance and pesticide production do not provide a benefit to consumers. Research continues to be done on crops that are useful for producers, for example, those that increase yields and can be cultivated under marginal conditions, such as drought-resistant and saline-tolerant crops. However, GM crops currently in development or under consideration also include traits that would primarily benefit consumers, such as nutritional enhancements. For example, golden rice is genetically engineered to produce betacarotene, the precursor to vitamin A, which is otherwise present in only trace amounts in rice. This is significant because, as discussed in Chapter 2, vitamin A deficiency is a widespread and severe problem that results in hundreds of thousands of children going blind and dying each year, many of whom live in places where rice is a staple food. Other GM organisms, while not themselves crops, are being developed to help with agricultural processing—e.g. microbes engineered to help to convert cellulose to biofuels—or use genomic materials from crop plants to produce what had formerly been agricultural products—e.g. the yeast engineered to produce artemisinic acid using wormwood genes.

It is estimated that in the United States revenues from genetically modified products—crops, biologics and industrial biotechnologies—exceeded $350 billion USD and constituted approximately 2.5% of the Gross Domestic Product in 2012 (Carlson, 2014). In 2013, 93% of the planted acreage of soybeans in the United States was genetically modified, as were over three-quarters of the planted acreage of corn and cotton. It is estimated that, globally, 79% of the planted acreage of soybeans, 70% of the acreage of cotton, and 32% of the acreage of corn were genetically modified (James, 2013). The United States, Brazil, Argentina, India and Canada are the largest adopters of GM crops. In total, GM crops are cultivated in 27 countries by an estimated 18 million farmers, and more biotech crop acreage is now planted in developing countries than in industrialized countries (James, 2013). If you live in a place where foodstuffs containing GM crops are not prohibited, and you do not actively avoid consuming them, the odds are that you routinely eat foods containing genetically modified organisms (GMOs) and have done so for quite some time.

ARGUMENTS IN SUPPORT OF GENETICALLY MODIFIED CROPS

First-generation GM crops are commodity crops designed for large-scale, intensive monoculture using synthetic chemical inputs. They emerge from and are intended to advance global industrial agricultural systems. It is not surprising, then, that the primary argument for GM crops is a corollary to the *feed the world argument* offered in support of industrial food systems (discussed at length in Chapter 1). Here is a summary of that argument. We face an enormous agricultural challenge—feeding over 7 billion people a nutritionally adequate and culturally appropriate diet. Although we are currently failing to fully meet that challenge—842 million people are undernourished—technological innovation in agriculture and globalization of food distribution systems have allowed us to make enormous progress. In fact, due largely to technological innovation and diffusion, more calories are produced per person today in every region of the world than were produced 50 years ago, even though the amount of land under cultivation per person has dropped dramatically (due to population increases). Agricultural demand is projected to increase a further 60% to 120% over the coming decades due to changes in diet and population growth. There are not significant amounts of additional land to cultivate or fish stocks to access, and climate change and ecological degradation are going to make production more difficult in many places. Therefore, the only way to feed the world going forward—and to have any hope of doing so while leaving space and resources for other species—is to innovate and incorporate best practices and novel technologies to increase agricultural production while also eliminating inefficiencies and losses throughout the agro-food system. GM technologies are crucial for this. They allow us to more efficiently and precisely engineer desirable traits into agricultural plants, such as disease resistance, improved yield, nutritional enhancement, drought resistance, heat tolerance, and pest resistance. Thus, GM crops should be embraced on both humanitarian and ecological grounds.

The feed the world argument in favor of GM crops is often supplemented by several other arguments. One of these is the *innovation presumption argument*. According to this argument, people ought to be able to innovate and adopt technologies unless there is a compelling reason to prevent them from doing so—e.g. that they are harming others (this is sometimes referred to as the *harm principle*). The reason for this is that people are autonomous, independent, rational agents, and exercising and expressing their autonomy is part of living a good human life. Therefore, just as people ought to be able to associate with whomever they like (unless there is a compelling reason to restrict them from doing so), they ought to be able to express their autonomy however they like (unless there is a compelling reason to restrict them from doing so), including through technological innovation and adoption. The innovation presumption is also sometimes justified by an appeal to benefits. People in highly technologized countries live much longer, healthier, more comfortable lives than have people at any point in human history. A large part of the explanation for this is technological innovation and adoption, which requires openness to new techniques, processes and technologies. Applied to GM crops, the innovation presumption implies that people ought to be able to develop and make use of them unless there is strong justification for not allowing them to do so.

Another argument offered in defense of GM crops is the *argument from substantial equivalence.* This argument, which is particularly important in some regulatory contexts, focuses on the fact that the product of GM crops is virtually identical to that of their non-GM counterparts. The difference between GM crops and non-GM crops is only a few genes. This is much less than the difference found between conventional hybrids and their parents, and the GM process is much more precise than hybridization (or induced mutagenesis). Moreover, with first-generation GM crops, the traits that are genetically modified have to do with cultivation, not with the product. The grains, soybeans and cotton produced from GM plants are exactly the same as those produced from non-GM varieties in all the relevant functional and nutritional respects. That is, from the perspective of the consumer, the two should be regarded as equivalent.

Furthermore, there is at present no evidence that eating GM foods is unsafe, which should be expected, given substantial equivalence. GM crops have been on the market for years and have been widely and longitudinally consumed without any problematic public health issues arising. This may not be the case with all GM crops. For example, a GM soybean engineered for nutritional enhancement with a gene derived from a nut was found to cause an allergic reaction in some people with nut allergies. However, with respect to first-generation GM crops, indications are that they are safe to consume (Nicolia et al., 2013). This is the *argument from safety.*

The *argument from incremental change* also emphasizes the similarity between GM crops and their non-GM counterparts. As described earlier, GM technologies and synthetic genomics enable greater precision and possibilities in genetic alteration than can be accomplished by means of hybridization, grafting, selective breeding, or induced mutagenesis. They are, nevertheless, the same sort of things—techniques that enable intentionally modifying plant genomes for human purposes. Thus, they represent only an incremental change from prior modification techniques. Given this, and the fact that the other techniques are widely used and not ethically objectionable, there should not be anything problematic with genetic modification and synthetic biology. In fact, their greater precision should be seen as desirable.

The foregoing are the primary considerations offered in support of GM crops. Several other arguments have been made on behalf of GM crops in response to objections that have been raised against them. I discuss those later in this chapter.

RESPONSE TO THE FEED THE WORLD ARGUMENT: GM CROPS UNDERMINE FOOD SECURITY

The primary response to the feed the world argument is that industrial agriculture in general, and GM crops in particular, are not needed to meet our agricultural challenges. Adopting best practices in organic farming, eliminating waste and loss from the food supply, increasing efficient utilization of calories/nutrition, reducing population growth, and promoting a more equitable distribution of resources (including the elimination of extreme poverty) could meet them as well, while also promoting justice and sustainability. The arguments for this have been presented already (see Chapters 1 and 2). Many proponents of this view believe that GM crops, along with the industrialization of agriculture, actually decrease food security and agricultural capability in the long run.

One argument for this, discussed in Chapter 1, is that industrial monoculture undermines food sovereignty. Once farmers adopt industrial agriculture, they begin to have much greater capital costs and become dependent upon purchasing the requisite inputs, such as seed and fertilizer. They also become reliant upon being able to market their crops at a high enough price so that they can afford to buy food for themselves. GM crops epitomize this problem. They are patented, so it is illegal to save seeds for the following year, and they are designed for use with expensive chemical inputs, such as herbicide. Thus, they are incompatible with traditional polyculture, dramatically increase the control of transnational corporations over the seed supply, and disempower smallholding farmers by increasing their dependencies and vulnerabilities.

A second argument, also discussed in Chapter 1, is that industrial agriculture and GM crops are ecologically detrimental. GM crops are seen as intertwined with and as perpetuating intensive chemical agriculture, so they promote all the ecological problems associated with it—e.g. nitrogen eutrophication, water contamination, and elevated greenhouse gas emissions. There is also concern that

GM crops might hybridize with related wild varieties or spread beyond their fields and become ecologically disruptive.

A third argument is that industrial agriculture and GM crops undermine the agricultural resource base. The use of chemical inputs is thought to reduce crucial microbial life in soils. The lack of rotation, fallow, and cover crops depletes soil nutrients, thereby requiring increased fertilizer use. Commodity monoculture often uses water resources faster than they can be replenished. GM crops, in addition to perpetuating these problems, are thought to undermine agricultural sustainability in two other ways. One is that, while they might increase yields in the short term, the fact that they involve high-volume use of a general herbicide and pesticide quite quickly results in plant and insect populations with evolved resistance to them. The resulting "super weeds" and "super pests" require the innovation of yet another set of chemicals. This is sometimes called the *pesticide and herbicide treadmill* because the novel technologies never actually get us anywhere—we have to innovate just to stay in place. The worry is that, eventually, the rate of innovation will be outpaced by the rate of resistance development. Another way in which GM crops are thought to undermine agricultural sustainability is that they displace so many other seed varieties that there is a loss of genetic diversity in our agricultural systems. This is problematic because when conditions change or new pests or viruses arise, a genetically diverse set of crops (as well as genetic diversity within crops) is crucial for adaptation. For example, Panama disease is rapidly spreading through the banana industry in Central America in part because the plants are genetically identical. Moreover, if genetically diverse types of seeds are altogether lost— not just no longer cultivated—it will be difficult to breed new, resistant or well-adapted varieties. It is for this reason that there are several major national and international initiatives to preserve traditional seed varieties—e.g. the Svalbard seed vault in Norway.

Many of the claims in the feed the world argument and the responses to it are empirical. For example, they concern what the impacts of industrial agriculture are now and will likely be in the future, as well as whether organic agriculture has the capacity to meet global food demand. Many of these contested claims were discussed in Chapter 1. The science around GM crops is also highly contested, but the research does favor one important conclusion:

different GM crops have different agricultural and ecological profiles. For example, it appears that cultivation of herbicide-resistant GM crops often results in increased herbicide usage. However, the use of GM Bt crops often reduces the amount of pesticide on the field, as well as its spread to adjacent areas (because it is produced by the plants rather than sprayed on) (Fernandez-Cornejo and McBride, 2000). The effects of GM crops on biodiversity also appear to vary. For some crops, insect and bird diversity is higher in conventional non-GM fields than in GM fields; for others, it is not (DEFRA, 2005). Variance is the theme with containment as well. Some GM crops have been documented to spread far afield, and some have characteristics that make them particularly likely to become ecologically problematic, such as high fecundity and her-bicide resistance. This is the case with GM creeping bentgrass—an herbicide-resistant grass created for use on golf courses. Other GM crops have not been documented as travelling very far and do not have high-risk characteristics. I discuss the differential ecological profiles of GM crops, and its significance for ethics, at greater length later in this chapter.

RESPONSE TO THE INNOVATION PRESUMPTION: THE PRECAUTIONARY PRINCIPLE

The innovation presumption is that we ought to allow agricultural innovation, including genetic modification, so long as there is not a compelling reason to restrict it. Critics of GM crops believe that, even if there is an innovation presumption, it is overcome by the detrimental ecological, agricultural and social impacts of GM crops described above (and discussed further below). Moreover, many critics of GM crops deny that there should be an innovation pre-sumption in the first place. Instead, they defend what is commonly known as the *precautionary principle*.

The basic idea of the precautionary principle is that when there is scientific uncertainty about risk, rather than presuming something is acceptable unless it is shown to be otherwise, it should be restricted until it is demonstrated to be safe. It reverses the presumption from acceptable until proven problematic (innovation presumption) to unacceptable until proven unproblematic (precautionary principle). There are myriad formulations of the precautionary principle, but when applied to GM crops, a formulation known as the Wingspread Statement is often invoked: "Where an activity raises threats of harm to the environment or human health, precautionary measures should be taken even if some cause and effect relationships are not fully established scientifically." The implication of this principle for GM crops is that they should be restricted until adequate safety to human health and the environment is established. The Wingspread formulation of the precautionary principle is conservative. It does not just say that it is permissible to take precautionary measures if there are possible threats. It says that such measures *should* be taken. Other formulations do not require taking action (only permit it), specify that action should only be taken if the risks are quite serious, or allow countervailing considerations against taking measures. One formulation along these lines is from the 1992 United Nations Rio Declaration on Environment and Development: "In order to protect the environment, the precautionary approach shall be widely applied by States according to their capabilities. Where there are threats of serious or irreversible damage, lack of full scientific certainty shall not be used as a reason for postponing cost-effective measures to prevent environmental degradation." The standard for restricting new technologies based on the Rio formulation is much higher than that of the Wingspread formulation—the threats must be serious and the measures must be cost-effective, for example. Still, some GM critics might argue that the concerns about GM crops are sufficient to meet the Rio threshold. (The Cartagena Protocol on Biosafety contains yet another formulation of the precautionary principle that has been influential in the GMO discourse.)

These two formulations of the precautionary principle illustrate that there is no such thing as the precautionary principle as such. Instead, there are a range of views—from the conservative Wingspread precautionary principle to the techno-optimism of the innovation presumption—on how much caution and how much confidence we should have with respect to technological innovation. All policy-making and all technological innovation and implementation take place under at least some level of uncertainty, since information is never perfect and since they aim to impact the future. Thus, a perennial issue in the ethics of emerging technologies is determining, in particular contexts and for particular technologies or issues, how much precaution is appropriate. This can depend upon a number of factors:

- *Features of the risk*—What is the magnitude of the risk? What is the probability it will occur? Is it reversible? How is the risk distributed/who is exposed to it?
- *Features of the uncertainty*—What is the level of uncertainty? What is required to reduce the uncertainty? How long would it take and how much less certainty would there be?
- *Features of the technology*—What benefits would the technology provide? How likely are those to accrue? What is their magnitude? How would they be distributed?
- *Features of the response*—What are the costs of implementing and enforcing controls/restrictions? What sorts of controls are required and would they be voluntary or mandatory? How much do they reduce the risk?
- *Features of the context*—What are cultural attitudes toward risk in this area? What is the capacity for implementing and enforcing controls? Do special or extenuating circumstances obtain?

Given these factors, the same amount of precaution may not be appropriate in all cases. For example, in the United States there is a high level of precaution with respect to drugs and devices. They require pre-market approval to demonstrate that they are both safe and effective, and they must be prescribed by a licensed physician in most instances. However, dietary supplements, largely due to a congressionally mandated exemption, do not require pre-market approval and are sold over the counter. For them, oversight is in the form of market acceptability, tort liability, and recalls if problems arise. Moreover, special circumstances obtain for experimental drugs and procedures to treat terminal patients, and there are calls to make them available even if there are high levels of uncertainty about their risks and effectiveness. Differential responsiveness to risk also occurs with respect to chemical policy. The EU has begun to implement a strict pre-market approval process, sometimes referred to as "no data, no market," for new chemicals, whereas the United States has a pre-market approval process for some chemicals (including pesticides), but not others.

The point here is not that all these policies are equally justified. It is that there are a range of possibilities for responding to risk and uncertainty, and that the appropriate level of caution need not be the same for all cases or all contexts. For example, people in France have different attitudes toward risks regarding dairy products (for cultural and aesthetic reasons) than do people in the United States, and this may justify different policies regarding raw milk products. The implication for GM crops is that not all GM crops in all locations must be treated the same. As we have already seen, different crops have different benefits and risks, with different levels of uncertainty, and they distribute these in different ways. They empower and disempower different actors. They are implemented in different cultural contexts, some of which are more accommodating of innovation (or bioengineering) in food and agriculture than others and have differential capacities to regulate GM crops.

In fact, that a crop is genetically modified by means of recombinant DNA techniques or synthetic biology provides only a small piece of information relevant to evaluating how much precaution is warranted. Compare, for example, Bt and herbicide-resistant corn to golden rice. The former does not directly benefit consumers and is nutritionally equivalent to non-GM corn. It is owned and controlled by large corporations that are very aggressive and litigious in defending their patents, and it is intertwined with chemical, industrial monoculture. In contrast, golden rice is intended to address a serious global health problem and benefit the world's worst-off people (those who suffer from malnutrition). It was developed by researchers at the Swiss Federal Institute of Technology and has received humanitarian exemptions on the patents involved. It is being hybridized into locally favored seed varieties that will be given away free (or at very low cost) to those in need, and it is not dependent upon industrial monoculture.

The foregoing suggests that differential evaluation and response to the risks associated with GM crops is often warranted. In fact, current regulations regarding GM crops reflect this. In the United States, GM crops are regarded by the federal government as substantially equivalent to their non-GM counterparts, so they do not need pre-market approval before entering the food supply and foods containing them do not need to be labeled. (The labeling issue is discussed below.) However, a significant amount of scientific data and field testing are required before they can be commercially cultivated. Thus, there is a somewhat precautionary approach to the environmental impacts of GM crops in the United States. (Proponents of GM crops often argue that even this is too precautionary, since it makes the barrier for market entry so high that only large-scale commercial crops developed by large corporations are economically feasible. The result is consolidation of control of the technology by those corporations, as well as exclusion of crops that would be beneficial to smaller growers and those with fewer resources. Thus, on this view, the greater precaution supported by critics of GM crops results in precisely the technologies and power relationships of which they are most critical.) In contrast, the EU currently allows member states to prohibit cultivation of GM crops, which many do, and requires that any foods containing GMOs be labeled. This is a much more precautionary approach than in the United States. Moreover, *differential assessment*—evaluating the risks of GM crops on a case-by-case basis—is part of GM policy not only in the United States, but also in New Zealand, the UK and Australia, for example, and has been advocated by the United Nations Food and Agricultural Organization (FAO, 2004).

RESPONSE TO THE ARGUMENT FROM SUBSTANTIAL EQUIVALENCE: PRODUCT VS. PROCESS

The argument from substantial equivalence claims that because the product of GM crops—the food component—is essentially identical to that produced by non-GM crops, GM crops should not be considered any different from an ethical or regulatory perspective. As discussed above, GM plants are not always substantially equivalent to their non-GM counterparts—e.g. the soybeans engineered with DNA from brazil nuts contained a potential allergen that non-GM soybeans lack. But in other cases, substantial equivalence does seem to hold. Bt corn is essentially indistinguishable as a foodstuff from non-Bt corn. However, critics of GM crops argue, it does not follow from substantial equivalence that GM crops should be regarded as identical to non-GM crops from an ethical or regulatory perspective, since the product of a process is not the only thing relevant to its evaluation. The process itself is often relevant. A clear non-food example of this is coerced or exploited labor to produce clothing. The product—the garments or shoes—might be substantially equivalent whether they are produced in a sweatshop or by workers receiving a fair wage under adequate working conditions. However, there is still a difference relevant to whether we ought to purchase or permit them. In fact, evaluation of process is common with food. "Fair trade," "free range" and "humanely produced" refer to ethical concerns about production processes. Therefore, even if the product of a GM crop is substantially equivalent to that of a non-GM crop, there could be features of the modification or how the crop is used that distinguish it ethically from a conventional crop.

RESPONSE TO THE ARGUMENT FROM INCREMENTAL CHANGE: DIFFERENCES IN DEGREE AND DIFFERENCES IN KIND

The argument from incremental change contends that genetic modification by recombinant DNA techniques and synthetic genomics are not radically new. They are just more precise and expansive ways of bioengineering organisms for agriculture, something that has been going on for millennia. This argument assumes that if something is only a change in degree, not a change in kind, from something ethically acceptable, it too should be ethically acceptable. However, this assumption is problematic. Differences in degree very often warrant differential ethical evaluation. Sending a child to her room for five minutes can be an appropriate punishment, sending her there for two days is child abuse. The difference is "only" a matter of degree, length of time, but it makes an ethical difference. Good-humored joking differs "only" in degree from ridicule, strict dieting differs "only" in degree from anorexia, and torture differs "only" in degree from interrogation. Identifying a property of something, even a crucial one, and showing that it differs only in degree from some ethically unproblematic object or practice does not establish that it is also unproblematic. The difference in degree may be ethically significant, or there may be other properties that are relevant to ethical evaluation. Thus, the fact that the methods of modifying GM crops differ only in degree from their predecessors does not imply that it should be regarded as ethically acceptable. The technology needs to be assessed directly, not only on the basis of how similar it is to what came before it.

EXTRINSIC OBJECTIONS TO GM CROPS

It is common in the ethics of bioengineering (and in technology ethics more generally) to distinguish between intrinsic objections and extrinsic objections. *Extrinsic objections* to a technology are objections based on the expected or possible outcomes or consequences of it. *Intrinsic objections* are based on the features of the technology itself, independent of whether its consequences are good or bad. GM crops are subject to both intrinsic and extrinsic objections. The extrinsic objections to GM crops concern their impacts on farmers, consumers and the environment. Here are the most prominent ones.

1. GM crops are not safe (or have not been adequately proven to be safe) for consumers—e.g. they might contain allergens, viruses are used in their development, and they might increase the amount of chemical residue on foods.
2. People are being used as "guinea pigs" for GM crops, violating their right to informed consent, since products containing them are not always labeled and have not been adequately studied for human health effects.
3. GM crops encourage intensive, agrichemical monoculture and thereby the problems associated with that form of agriculture—e.g. nutrient depletion, chemical pollution, overuse of water, and desertification.
4. GM crops are detrimental to natural biodiversity by encouraging the use of synthetic chemicals, through unintended gene flow from GM plants to wild species, and by the unintended dispersal of GM crops into natural ecosystems where they might outcompete wild species.
5. GM crops are likely to foster the creation of super weeds and super pests that are resistant to pesticides, herbicides and traditional crop protection techniques.
6. GM crops are a *technofix* for our agricultural challenges, which have largely been caused by industrial commodity monoculture. They not only fail to address the causes of our agricultural problems, but emerge from and perpetuate the system that helps to create them.
7. GM crops discourage genetic diversity within crops, as well as diversity of crops, and thereby threaten food security.

8. GM crops encourage control of agriculture and food production by a small number of powerful transnational seed corporations.

9. GM crops encourage a global commodity-based agricultural economy that is advantageous to the wealthy—corporations and those who can afford the technologies—and that marginalizes and disempowers smallholding farmers.

10. GM crops are part of the undemocratic push for globalization and homogenization that threatens cultural difference, erodes national sovereignty, and undermines environmental and worker protections.

11. GM crops will not be effective in providing nutritional adequacy to people who do not currently have it, and they will undermine food security in the long run because of their connection to commodity monoculture.

12. GM crops are detrimental to traditional polyculture and the people and communities who practice it, since their use displaces traditional farming methods and cultural practices.

13. GM crops are not cost-effective. The economic and ecological costs of using them, particularly for smallholding farmers, outweigh the value of the purported gains in yield, which are themselves exaggerated.

The vast majority of these concerns trade on the relationship between GM crops and global industrial food systems (and commodity-based monoculture), the ecological impacts of GM crops, or the health and autonomy of consumers of GM crops. Almost all of these objections have already been discussed either earlier in this chapter or in the prior chapters on food systems and food security (Chapters 1 and 2). I will not repeat those discussions here, but will emphasize some key points related to their evaluation.

First, concerns based on the relationship between GM crops and industrial agriculture are only valid insofar as GM crops are intertwined with global industrial agriculture and perpetuate or fail to address the problems thought to be associated with it. As discussed above, this need not be the case with all GM crops. Even if they characterize first-generation GM crops—e.g. Bt and herbicide-resistant crops—they may not do so for all future crops, such as golden rice. Of course, these concerns also depend upon the validity of the criticisms of the global industrial food system and commodity monoculture. If those are not problematic, or if what problems they do have can be adequately addressed, then it is not an objection to GM crops when they are part of them.

With respect to the ecological impacts of GM crops, the discussion above regarding caution and confidence is crucial. GM crops involve modifying organisms and introducing them into ecological systems through cultivation and into people and animals through consumption. Predicting and controlling interventions into complex biological and ecological systems is often challenging—ecological containment, for instance, can be very difficult—and they often have detrimental unintended consequences. Therefore, it is important to have appropriate *humility* and to avoid *hubris*—i.e. to not overestimate our knowledge and control. However, as discussed above, it does not follow from this that very strong precaution is required with respect to all GM crops and in all cases, since different crops have different social, ethical, agricultural and ecological profiles.

Differential assessment is also necessary when evaluating the human welfare impacts of GM crops. The fact that a plant has been genetically modified by particular techniques provides very little information about its potential benefits, costs, risks, cultural situatedness, control, oversight or access. These are crucial to its impacts on well-being, rights, autonomy and power, which in turn are central to determining whether its use is compassionate, ecologically sensitive, just and respectful.

INTRINSIC OBJECTIONS TO GM CROPS

Intrinsic objections to GM crops are objections to them *as such*. Many people believe that intentionally creating transgenic or interspecific individuals is wrong, independent of the consequences or outcomes of doing so. As discussed earlier, intentional genetic hybridization across species is common and unobjectionable when done by traditional breeding techniques. Moreover, if engineering organisms were itself objectionable, virtually all of our food supply and all of our companion animals (and house plants) would be ethically problematic. The concern with bioengineering GM crops (and animals) is that it involves mixing genomic material of species to create novel life-forms that could not have existed in the absence of human agency. It is, therefore, charged with being unnatural, hubristic, and playing God. In this section, I discuss these three prominent intrinsic objections to GM crops.

The term "natural" is ambiguous. It is sometimes used to refer to everything in the physical world—that is, everything that acts according to the laws of nature. Other times, it refers only to the biological or ecological world. Still other times, it is used to refer to everything in the world that is neither human nor the product of human agency. Therefore, whether GM crops are *unnatural* depends upon which meaning of the term is operative. They are part of the physical world, and in that sense natural. They are a modified part of the biological world, so in that sense partially natural. They are created and used by humans, so in that sense unnatural.

However, the fact that GM crops are unnatural in the sense of being the product of human agency does not make them unethical. If it did, then cars, phones, yogurt and Chihuahuas would all be ethically objectionable. All engineering and technology involves modifying things or creating things not found in nature. Moreover, we are technological animals. Intentionally modifying the world is crucial to our form of life. We cannot equate something's being the product of human agency with its being unethical.

The foregoing is an argument from cases, and it is a *reductio ad absurdum*. That is, it aims to show that if you accept the principle "if something is the product of human agency and could not have otherwise existed, then it is objectionable," the implications are absurd, since it would evaluate things that are clearly not ethically problematic as ethically problematic. However, there is also a deeper conceptual problem with the evaluative use of "natural": nature is not normative for us. We have already seen that the fact that something is not found in nature or does not occur in nature does not make it wrong for us to do or create. In addition to this, the fact that something is found or occurs in nature does not make it permissible for us to do. The biological world is characterized by predation; deception is commonplace; forced copulation occurs in many species; and parents only very rarely raise or protect their offspring. Thus, whether or not something occurs in nature is not normative or prescriptive for us. To take nature as normative commits the *fallacy of appeal to nature* discussed in the previous chapter.

Proponents of the unnaturalness objection to GM crops often respond to these sorts of arguments by claiming that we should not follow all of nature, just the appropriate parts of it, or that not all of our actions are unnatural, just the problematic ones. However, these responses depend upon having a standard other than naturalness for determining when and in what ways "natural" is prescriptive. That is, the normative content comes from criteria outside the concept of "natural." When pushed to explain what the criteria might be, proponents of the unnaturalness objection very often fall back on either extrinsic concerns, particularly potential impacts on ecological systems, or theological concerns usually having to do with the sanctity of species boundaries. That is, they sometimes claim that the creation of GMOs involves "playing God."

Human beings cannot literally play God. If God exists, God's knowledge and power so far outstrip ours that we cannot simulate God. Therefore, the idea of "playing God" must be understood metaphorically. Typically, it is meant to refer to things that are beyond the appropriate use of our agency. We are playing God when we genetically engineer organisms because, although we are capable of doing it, it is not the sort of thing we ought to be involved in. It goes beyond the appropriate purview of our agency. However, this view, like that of GM crops being unnatural, *begs the question*. What defines the purview of appropriate agency? Why are hybridization and selective breeding within it, but genetic engineering and synthetic genomics outside it?

Non-theological versions of the playing-God objection typically appeal to extrinsic concerns to answer this question. It is playing God because there are risks involved that we do not fully understand or to which we are not adequately attending. As a result, we are being hubristic. They also sometimes appeal to the naturally evolved *telos* of organisms—i.e. that plants have certain ends or goals that are the result of human independent evolutionary processes and with which genetic engineering interferes. This, it should be clear, is an instance of appeal to the normativity of "natural" and commits the fallacy of appeal to nature. It is also difficult to see why genetic engineering should interfere with a plant's (or animal's) telos, if it has one, more so than does hybridization. Moreover, GM plants are not non-GM plants that are then turned into GM plants. They are GM plants from their inception—so it is not the case that they had one set of ends or goals that were then modified or disrupted.

Theological versions of the playing-God objection to GM crops typically appeal to divinely prescribed species boundaries, which GM crops violate. Notice, however, that this objection has gone from being ethical to being religious. Moreover, it should be noted that almost all religious traditions allow for genetic hybridization across species, and many religious leaders have come to accept or even support GM crops (the Vatican, for example).

In addition to being unnatural and playing God, GM crops are often charged with being hubristic. Those who develop them and promote their use are seen as lacking proper humility. There are actually several different concerns relating to the hubris charge:

1. Development and cultivation of GM crops involve over-estimation of our ability to predict and control the impacts of our innovations in complex biological and ecological systems.
2. GM crops are a technofix for our agricultural and ecological problems; rather than addressing the causes of the problems, they treat the problematic effects while perpetuating their source (industrial agriculture).
3. The pursuit of biotechnology, including GM crops, is done for our own aggrandizement and to achieve mastery over nature.
4. Biotechnology, including GM crops, takes a reductionist view of life, seeing biological organisms as genetic pieces or commodities for us to reconfigure for our own ends.

The first two of these concerns are variations of extrinsic concerns about the relationship of GM crops to industrial agriculture, as well as the risks involved with pursuing them. I discussed these earlier in this chapter. I suggested that even if they are applicable to most currently cultivated GM crops, they need not be for all future GM crops. If this is correct, then they will not support intrinsic objections to GM crops, since they do not apply to them as such.

The third concern involves empirical claims about the motives and intentions of people who engage in GM research. I am not aware of any research that supports these claims. There are certainly people involved in genomics research who are arrogant and say hubristic things, such as "we are moving from reading the genetic code to writing it." However, there are also many people who are both well intentioned and deeply concerned about developing the technology in responsible ways. It is not a necessary feature of the pursuit of biotechnologies that those who do so are hubristic.

With respect to the fourth concern, it is certainly true that genomic engineering is reductionist in many ways. It involves understanding discrete genetic components, as well as altering organisms at their "basic" genomic level in as precise a way as possible. However, it does not follow from this that people engaged in the research (or that use GM crops) see life-forms as mere commodities or sources of genetic material, rather than as entities that can be valuable and worthy of respect. Nor does it follow that they see genetic engineering as a way to reengineer the biological world to our own ends writ large. In fact, many researchers and advocates of genetic engineering are motivated in part by a desire to reduce our ecological impacts and protect more resources for other species. Therefore, as with the other hubris concerns, this one seems to have some validity, but to apply only in some cases or to some researchers. Therefore, it is not an objection to GM technologies as such.

LABELING

One of the most contested issues surrounding GM crops concerns labeling foods containing them. Labeling is currently mandatory in the EU, and there have been several state-level votes on the issue in the United States. (It has passed in some cases, failed in others.) Over two-thirds of processed foods in the United States contain GMOs, so mandatory labeling would have far-reaching implications.

It is useful to distinguish between positive and negative labeling, as well as voluntary and mandatory labeling. *Positive labeling* indicates the presence of something—in this case, that the product contains GMOs—whereas *negative labeling* indicates the absence of something—in this case, that the product does not contain GMOs. *Mandatory labeling* is labeling required by law or regulation, whereas *voluntary labeling* is labeling done at the discretion of the producer, manufacturer or vendor.

The core arguments in support of mandatory labeling of foods containing GMOs appeal to consumer autonomy—i.e. people have a right to know what is in the food that they eat. One reason people need to know about their food is so that they can make informed decisions regarding safety and health. This is why many countries require labeling for major allergens, ingredients and nutrition. Proponents of GM labeling believe that this justification applies to GMOs on the basis of the safety and health concerns discussed above. They also argue that people need to know about the presence of GMOs so that they can act on the basis of any ethical or religious views they might have about them.

In response, opponents of labeling appeal to substantial equivalence, arguing that if GM and non-GM crops are aesthetically and nutritionally identical, there is no need for labeling. In fact, given substantial equivalence, labeling suggests that there is a difference when there is not. So rather than being informative, labeling promotes false beliefs and unjustified stigma against products containing GMOs. This last consideration is sometimes used to argue against even voluntary negative labeling—i.e. labels of the form "This product does not contain GMOs."

Proponents of labeling often reply to this by pointing out that informational labeling is not restricted to the content of foods. Mandatory labeling often includes information about country of origin, location of processing, and other aspects of foods that people care about. Therefore, if people care enough about the presence of GMOs in their food, then labeling should be required, whether or not there is substantial equivalence.

In addition to appeals to substantial equivalence and unjustified stigma, opponents of labeling often argue against it on the grounds that it will make food more expensive. It will require careful separation of GM from non-GM commodities, as well as verification and enforcement across food supply chains. Opponents of labeling estimate that mandatory labeling could increase food costs by several hundred dollars per year for consumers in the United States, which is a significant increase for households that are food insecure. Moreover, it passes on these costs to all consumers, regardless of whether they care about the presence of GMOs in their food. In contrast, the costs associated with voluntary negative labeling, including certified organic labeling, are targeted. Those who care about the presence of GMOs can choose to pay more for foods that are labeled as non-GMO (or organic). Of course, for those who are food insecure, this may not be an economically viable option. (Not surprisingly, labeling proponents believe that the claims about cost increases associated with mandatory labeling are dramatically overstated.)

People care about a great many things when it comes to choosing food, but it is not possible, logistically or economically, to put everything everyone cares about on every package. There is general consensus that safety-relevant information should be mandatory. However, beyond safety, there is a tremendous divergence in views, both within and between countries, on what should be required. Moreover, in recent years there has been a proliferation of voluntary labeling, including third party certifications, on the basis of ethical concerns about such things as fair trade, worker rights, animal welfare, farming methods and ecological impacts. There are now over 200 different kinds of eco-labels alone. Therefore, determining how decisions about mandatory labeling should be made, as well as how to ensure accuracy (and permissibility) in voluntary labeling, are increasingly important issues in food ethics. (The ethics of labeling is discussed further in Chapter 5.)

GENETICALLY MODIFIED ANIMALS

The motivations for genetically engineering animals are the same as for conventional animal engineering (e.g. selective breeding)—to improve the production process and/or the quality of the product. For example, AquAdvantage© salmon are Atlantic salmon engineered with ocean pout and Chinook salmon genes that cause them to grow year-round rather than seasonally, halving their time to market. Enviropig© swine are engineered so that they produce an enzyme in their saliva that results in their having less phosphorus in their waste. Livestock cloning has largely been used on breeding animals with desirable fertility and meat characteristics.

Almost all of the arguments for and concerns about GM crops apply, in appropriately modified form, to GM animals. For example, one of the main arguments for GM salmon is that increased aquaculture production capacity is needed to meet global demand for fish protein, which is an instance of the feed the world argument, while one of the primary concerns about them is that they will escape and have detrimental ecological impacts, which mirrors the ecological concern associated with the unintended dispersal of

GM crops. Similarly, the reduced phosphorous waste argument for Enviropig© is analogous in many respects to the reduced pesticide use argument for Bt crops, while one of the main arguments against Enviropig© is that it is a technofix that would perpetuate CAFO animal production, just as one of the core arguments against herbicide-resistant crops is that they are a technofix that perpetuates chemical-intensive commodity monoculture.

There are a few important differences between bioengineering crops and bioengineering animals. One is that there are greater levels of public concern about and resistance to the creation and consumption of GM animals. However, this alone does not mean that GM animals are more ethically problematic. It is important not to commit the *fallacy of appeal to the crowd*. That a large number of people believe something is problematic or repugnant does not make it so. Not long ago, there was widespread opposition to in vitro fertilization as well as to interracial marriage. Our moral responses and judgments can be the product of false beliefs, biases, inconsistent reasoning and lack of understanding, for example. This is why engaging in careful, well-informed, and well-reasoned ethical reflection is so crucial. It is how individual and social ethical progress is made.

Nevertheless, the fact that people have a stronger response to GM animals than to GM crops does invite the question: is there any ethically relevant difference between plant bioengineering and animal bioengineering that could justify it? There is, of course, one important difference between plants and animals: only the latter have psychological experiences and can feel pain. On an animal rights view, the implication of this is that animals should not be treated as mere things to be used for our ends. Therefore, creating and raising genetically engineered animals for human consumption is unethical (just as it is for non-GM animals), since it involves manipulating them for our own ends and using them for our purposes.

On an animal welfare view of the moral status of animals, evaluation of genetic engineering is more complex. The reason for this is that it might be possible to genetically modify animals in ways that would reduce the suffering associated with animal agriculture, particularly with CAFOs. For example, it has been suggested that chickens could be engineered to be blind, since blind chickens are more docile and may not require debeaking, a tremendously painful process; it has been suggested that turkeys could be engineered to not have brooding impulses, which are frustrated in CAFOs; and it has been suggested that genetic engineering could be used to remove boar taint, thereby eliminating the "need" for castration. Researchers are also interested in engineering animals that are less susceptible to diseases and parasites. There is even research on engineering microencephalic pigs and chickens that have brain function that is sufficient for maintaining growth but not for supporting mental states or psychological experiences. If achieved, these animals would not suffer at all, regardless of how they are treated.

There are two common critical responses to these sorts of proposals for reducing animals' suffering. One is that they are technofixes. The fact that it could be better to be a microencephalic pig or a blind chicken than a normally functioning one in a CAFO demonstrates just how problematic CAFOs are from an animal welfare perspective. Moreover, these "solutions" do not address the cause of the problem—the form of agriculture—but treat only one problematic aspect of it and/or to only some extent. Even if it is better for chickens to be blind than have sight in CAFOs, it is still bad for them to be there. The rest of the mistreatments persist—the problematic diets, space, hormones, diseases and reproduction—and they are also blind. The better option is to eliminate the cause of the suffering, the CAFOs themselves, not to find ways that partially address the suffering involved and that would give the illusion of CAFOs being acceptable from an animal welfare perspective.

The second response to proposals to engineer animals to improve their welfare is that it is not likely to successfully reduce animal suffering. One reason for this is that the modifications might not work as intended—e.g. cognitively diminished pigs might still suffer, and it might be more difficult for us to know that they do. A second reason is that there may be unanticipated consequences. For example, blind chickens, although more docile than sighted chickens, may have more accidents and broken bones. Or it might make it possible to further intensify production of them—to have more chickens per unit of space—such that even if each chicken suffers somewhat less, there is as much or more suffering in aggregate.

Critics of GM animals believe that proposals to address animal welfare through genetic engineering are in an untenable position. They recognize that animal suffering caused by CAFOs is ethically problematic and that it needs to be addressed. However, once this is recognized, it is clear that the ethically responsible thing to do is to eliminate CAFOs. The arguments for engineering animals on animal welfare grounds are therefore seen as committing the *false dilemma fallacy*. The choice is not only between CAFOs with non-GM animals and CAFOs with GM animals, since eliminating CAFOs must also be considered.

Not all genetic engineering of animals is intended to address animal welfare or ecological concerns associated with industrial production processes. More often, it is done to improve the animal from a production and product standpoint—to make it grow faster, taste better, or be less costly. This raises concerns from an animal welfare perspective, since most animal welfare issues are the result of selecting for traits and production processes that aim at increasing efficiency and reducing cost per unit. Engineering chickens that have even larger breasts, cows that produce even more milk, cattle that grow even faster, and animals that are even more docile are likely to increase abnormalities, health problems, mistreatment and thereby suffering in CAFOs. For example, AquAdvantage© salmon have an increased risk of jaw deformities, and animals that are engineered to be resistant to diseases and parasites could be kept in even higher densities. In addition, the engineering process itself raises animal welfare concerns. For example, extracting eggs and implanting genetically engineered embryos have risks and cause suffering. Moreover, success rates, particularly at the start, are very low, and offspring often have health problems ranging from disease susceptibility to vascular and muscular abnormalities.

Overall, the main difference between ethical evaluation of genetically engineering animals and genetically engineering plants is that animal welfare must be considered. On most animal rights views, the creation and use of GM animals for human consumption is unethical. On animal welfare views, case-by-case evaluation is needed, since it is possible that some instances of genetic engineering will have a positive impact on animal welfare. However, when alternatives to CAFOs are considered, it is difficult to identify genetic modifications that would reduce animal suffering enough to make CAFOs acceptable from an animal welfare perspective.

SYNTHETIC MEAT

Meat is animal tissue, and animal tissue is standardly grown on animals. However, it is also possible to grow animal tissue *ex vivo* using cell cultures with growth promoters and nutritional media. This has been done in research contexts for decades. The core idea behind cultured meat is to scale up and industrialize this process, so that large amounts of animal tissue is grown for human consumption "off the hoof" and without the impacts of animal agriculture. There is significant support for cultured meat. The animal rights organization PETA—People for the Ethical Treatment of Animals—is offering a one-million-dollar prize for the first cultured meat product that comes to market. Dozens of research groups are working to develop in vitro meat, and there has been some limited success. At a recent event in London, cultured meat patties were cooked and eaten.

The core ethical concerns about eating meat are that industrial animal agriculture causes large amounts of suffering and has enormous ecological impacts. Both of these concerns are associated with the fact that the meat we eat is gotten from animals, which have the capacity to suffer and inefficiently convert feed calories and nutrition into edible tissue while also producing large amounts of waste. (The animal welfare and ecological concerns about meat production were discussed at length in Chapter 3.) If animals were eliminated from industrial meat production, then perhaps it would not be as ethically problematic. This is the core argument in favor of bioengineering synthetic, artificial, in vitro or cultured meat.

The motivations for cultured meat are ethical, eliminating the suffering and ecological impacts associated with animal agriculture. It is not being pursued for economic reasons, to meet public demand for synthetic meat, or for aesthetic (taste) reasons. In fact, these are among the largest barriers to its success. Regarding cost, industrially produced animal meat is inexpensive, particularly in ground and processed forms. Synthetic meat is unlikely to produce high-end cuts of meat (for reasons discussed below), so to be economically competitive it needs to be at the processed and ground meat price point. Moreover, industrial animal agriculture is critical to a wide variety of industries, such as leather and pet food, and animal parts find their way into a great many products, from cleaners to cigarettes. This is crucial to the economic profile of industrial animal agriculture. Cultured meat, since it produces only animal tissue, cannot substitute for industrial animal agriculture throughout the animal product system, and this renders making it cost comparable more challenging.

Regarding aesthetics, one the challenges for the commercial development of cultured meat is growing it so that it has a taste and texture similar to meat grown "on the hoof." Taste and texture are products of tissue type, as well as the conditions of growth—e.g. nutritional inputs, stress and stimulation. Animal muscle tissue has to do work, and there are all sorts of metabolic processes impacting it. This is crucial to its fibrousness and muscle-to-fat ratios, for example. How to simulate these processes and conditions to get similar-tasting and similar-textured tissue out of a bioreactor is a difficult problem for cultured meat researchers. It has been suggested that rather than try to mimic meat grown on the hoof, cultured meat should aim for its own aesthetics. The thought is that if it tastes good enough, people will eat it even if it does not taste like meat. There is an analog to this in meat substitutes. Some non-meat "burgers" aim to mimic the flavor of meat, while others just aim to taste good and fill the dietary and culinary functions of meat. However, if cultured meat does not displace animal-grown meat, then it will not have the intended animal welfare and ecological benefits.

Regarding public demand, not only is there no clamor for cultured meat, there appears to be significant barriers to gaining market acceptance. As mentioned earlier, there is greater public concern regarding bioengineering animals than plants. There is significant public reluctance to eating meat from cloned animals. There was also a public outcry in the United States against "pink slime" (or lean finely textured beef) being served to school children, which is a processed meat product produced by heating and spinning the trimmings after butchering in order to extract the remaining tissue. Each of these involves resistance to non-standardly produced meat products that are derived from animals. Given this, it is reasonable to expect that there will be at least as much resistance to bioengineered meat that is grown in bioreactors. The challenge of public acceptance is compounded by the fact that cultured meat is likely to be more expensive and taste less good (or different) than meat grown on the hoof. This has led to speculation that, at best, cultured meat will become a niche product for affluent people who want to eat meat but who are concerned about the ethics of doing so.

It may be true that cultured meat is ethically preferable to meat grown on the hoof in CAFOs. It is likely to be more efficient, because all the inputs will go toward growing edible tissue rather than toward keeping the animal alive, growing hair and teeth, and fueling locomotion. It will not have any of the ecological impacts of the animal itself, such as waste and methane emissions. It will not directly cause animals to suffer, so long as the inputs are not derived from animals (currently, the primary cell growth medium used is fetal calf serum). However, the considerations above constitute significant practical barriers to cultured meat displacing meat produced through industrial animal agriculture. The argument for the pursuit of cultured meat may also commit the false dilemma fallacy. After all, the choice is not only between cultured meat and meat from industrial animal agriculture. There is also the option of meat from other sources, such as hunting or small organic farms, as well as adopting a meat-free diet. It is not urgent that cultured meat be developed as an alternative to CAFO meat. Widely available, good-tasting, inexpensive and healthy alternatives already exist.

The discussion above suggests that the ethical argument for cultured meat may not be as strong as it initially appears. But even if that is the case, it does not follow that developing cultured meat is problematic or wrong, particularly if there is merit to the innovation presumption. However, several objections to cultured meat have been raised.

One concern about cultured meat production is that for it to be commercially viable it would need to be a large-scale, centralized industrial process. The cultured meat vision is not (at present) for a distributed system in which people have their own bioreactors. Instead, it would involve large meat manufacturing facilities and extensive distribution systems, so it will be squarely located within the industrial food system paradigm. Those who find such a system problematic are therefore likely to object to cultured meat on the basis of its industrial features. It is an interesting aspect of cultured meat that it splits those who are opposed to industrial animal agriculture for animal welfare reasons from those who are opposed to it for systemic reasons, since it retains the industrialization, but without the animals.

A related concern about cultured meat is that it takes a reductionist approach to meat production. This is an instance of the slow food worry that industrialization of food and agricultural systems eliminates culture, tradition, skill, difference and context. It leads to food production being a form of manufacturing and to food consumption being focused on "fueling up." It alienates people from their food, hides the production process, and culturally (and spiritually) impoverishes food and agriculture. Of course, these same concerns are raised regarding industrial animal agriculture. The false dilemma issue discussed above is therefore important here, since the implication is that non-meat and alternative animal meat diets are preferable to diets high in either industrial animal meat or industrial cultured meat.

Yet another related concern about cultured meat is that it is a counterproductive half measure. If it is ethically wrong to eat animals, then it seems problematic to eat their approximation. Suppose that instead of culturing bovine or fowl tissue, someone were to culture human tissue for consumption. This would strike many as highly objectionable. Even if it did not involve actually eating another person, the fact that it is wrong to eat another person (which most people would agree upon) makes eating human tissue grown in vitro perverse. Moreover, the "need" for cultured meat seems to feed into the "can't go without meat narrative," which, as discussed in the previous chapter, is empirically false and problematically gendered. Furthermore, if the concerns raised in the prior paragraphs are valid, then eating cultured meat may make people feel as if they are acting ethically, even though it is a worse alternative than adopting a non-industrial-meat diet.

Cultured meat may be ethically preferable to meat produced through CAFOs. However, it may not be preferable to diets that do not include industrially produced meat at all. It may also have some ethically problematic dimensions, though perhaps not to such an extent that it overcomes the innovation presumption.

CONCLUSION

We depend upon bioengineering to feed ourselves. We do not cultivate wild plants or raise wild animals. Therefore, the issue is not whether to bioengineer plants and animals in the future, but how to do it ethically. A theme throughout this chapter has been that bioengineered agricultural organisms have diverse ethical profiles. They have different objectives, risks and benefits (and distributions of them); they have different power, control and access implications; and they are embedded within different agricultural systems. For these reasons, it is unlikely that either global endorsement or global opposition to GM plants and animals is justified. Therefore, it is crucial to attend to the particulars of the technologies and their contexts, as well as to the design of regulatory systems and policies, so as to encourage development of and access to agricultural biotechnologies that promote human flourishing and are just, sustainable, efficient and compassionate.

FURTHER READING

Several of the books on food systems and food ethics listed at the end of Chapter 1 address issues related to genetically modified organisms. Vandana Shiva's work on this topic (*Stolen Harvest*) has been particularly influential. Some books that focus specifically on the ethics of genetically engineering plants and animals include:

Michael Ruse and David Castle, eds., *Genetically Modified Foods: Debating Biotechnology* (Prometheus)

Britt Bailey and Marc Lappé, eds., *Engineering the Farm: Ethical and Social Aspects of Agricultural Biotechnology* (Island Press)

Paul Thompson, *Food Biotechnology in Ethical Perspective* (Springer)

Gary Comstock, *Vexing Nature? On the Ethical Case against Agricultural Biotechnology* (Springer)

Bernard Rollin, *The Frankenstein Syndrome: Ethical and Social Issues in the Genetic Engineering of Animals* (Cambridge University Press)

Ronald Sandler, *The Ethics of Species: An Introduction* (Cambridge University Press)

Two articles that greatly informed the discussion of synthetic meat in this chapter are:

Paul Thompson, "Artificial Meat," in *Ethics and Emerging Technologies* (Palgrave Macmillan)

Stella Welin, Julie Gold and Johanna Berlin, "In Vitro Meat: What are the Moral Issues?" in *The Philosophy of Food* (University of California Press)

FOOD AND HEALTH

Food is critical to good health. Without reliable access to adequate calories and nutrition, people do not develop and function well; they are more susceptible to illness and chronic diseases; and they can die. This was discussed at length in Chapter 2. Of course, food is related to health in other ways as well. There are hazards associated with food consumption—of foreign objects, pathogens and chemicals. Overconsumption of food and consumption of nutritionally poor foods can increase the risks of heart disease, diabetes and other illnesses for individuals, as well as pose serious public health challenges. Many people have food allergies, which can be quite severe. There are disorders around food, such as anorexia and bulimia. This chapter addresses the ethical dimensions of issues related to food and health.

FOODBORNE RISKS

Foodborne illness has a wide range of causes, including viruses, bacteria, parasites, toxins and prions. Some of the more common pathogens in affluent nations are *e. coli*, salmonella, norovirus, listeria and campylobacter. In the United States, an estimated 48 million U.S. citizens (or 1 in 6 people) get sick, 128,000 people are hospitalized, and 3,000 people die each year from foodborne illnesses.

In the UK, around a million people get sick, approximately 20,000 people are hospitalized, and 500 people die each year. In developing nations, the problem is much more severe. According to the World Health Organization, there are up to 2 billion cases of illness from food and water each year, and 1.6 million people die from diarrheal diseases each year, the majority of whom are children. A major reason for this is that 2.5 billion people live without adequate sanitation and that 768 million people lack dependable access to potable drinking water.

Food can become contaminated at virtually any point in the food system. It can occur in the field due to lack of sanitation or due to contaminated inputs, as has happened in recent years with spinach (*e. coli*) and tomatoes (salmonella) in North America. It can occur during processing and manufacture, as has been the case with outbreaks associated with infant formula in China. It can be caused by improper preparation, as was the case with a 1993 *e. coli* outbreak associated with undercooked meat at Jack in the Box restaurants in the United States. And it can happen during transportation and storage as a result of spoilage or pest infestation. Diseases can also spread among animals kept in close quarters—e.g. avian bird flu in Asia—or through the global animal trade—e.g. mad cow disease in the EU and Canada.

All types of food can become contaminated. It happens with both organically grown and conventionally grown foods, as well as with local foods and globally sourced and processed foods. However, the risks associated with all foods are not equal. Higher-risk foods include meat, eggs, dairy products, and raw foods. Higher-risk activities include eating in places where others prepare your food (e.g. eating out) or where there is not strong oversight and regulation (e.g. street vendors).

As mentioned above, foodborne illness is not the only food safety issue. Severe allergic reactions are also common. It is estimated that 17 million Europeans and 15 million Americans have food allergies. In the United States, 4% to 6% of children have food allergies, and there are more than 300,000 ambulatory care incidents and 200,000 emergency room visits each year associated with them (CDC, 2013). Synthetic chemicals such as PBDE, dioxins, DDT, xenoestrogen and BPA can contaminate foods in the field, in the wild, or during processing and manufacture, and they can accumulate in the body over time, thereby contributing to longitudinal health problems. Macroscale foreign objects are also sometimes found in both manufactured and freshly prepared foods.

The primary prescriptive questions associated with food safety are these:

- What level of risk is acceptable (that is, what is the minimum threshold for safety)? What level of risk should be the goal (that is, what is the ideal level of safety)?
- Who ought to be responsible for ensuring food safety? What is the distribution of responsibilities for consumers, retailers, suppliers, producers and regulators?
- What information relevant to food safety should be communicated to consumers, particularly in the form of labeling?
- What levels of precaution and confidence regarding food safety are appropriate regarding things as diverse as food additives, processing techniques, and nutritional supplements?

These questions are addressed in what follows.

NORMATIVE DIMENSIONS OF RISK

It is crucial to distinguish risk from safety. *Risk* is a quantitative measure of the frequency and magnitude of a hazard. For example, the risk of contracting salmonella from eating rare meat refers to the frequency with which this occurs, the number of incidents per consumption, as well as how bad it is when it occurs, the probabilistic range of outcomes. Although risk assessment is largely a scientific process, it nevertheless has ineliminable normative and thereby ethical components—e.g. in choosing what risks to assess, what measures to use in the assessments, how to count marginal cases, how to deal with uncertainty, what quality of data can be used, and what levels of confidence are sufficient for drawing conclusions. Risk assessment is not merely a matter of "crunching the numbers" or "running the stats," since it is often done on imperfect data, in real time, and with substantial unknowns.

For instance, nanomaterials are increasingly utilized in the food supply chain as additives, fillers and coatings, and in packaging, among other uses. For example, nanoscale titanium dioxide is used as a whitener and brightener in cottage cheese, candy, soy milk, mayonnaise and many other products. *Nanomaterials* refer to materials that are sized on the nanoscale, one billionth of a meter, which is the scale of individual atoms and molecules. They are exciting from an engineering standpoint because they often have different structural, chemical, electrical and tensile properties than their bulk counterparts; and different nanomaterials of the same substance can have very different properties. This diversity provides engineers, including those working in the food industry, which is on the leading edge of nanomaterials, with greater ability to innovate and improve products with respect to such things as taste, shelf life, tracking and monitoring. But the same features that make nanomaterials so promising from an engineering perspective also make it difficult to predict how they will behave in different combinations, concentrations and contexts, including in our bodies. It is not always reliable to generalize from the properties of their bulk counterparts. Thus, risk assessment of nanomaterials often involves making choices about such things as what data is applicable, how to extrapolate on the basis of that data, and how to respond to high levels of uncertainty. Novel nanomaterials are a particularly difficult case for risk assessment, given their diverse properties and the lack of information about them. However, these same types of normative judgments are a common part of food risk assessment. They arise with everything from artificial sweeteners to food containers, and from GMOs to defining overweight/obesity.

DETERMINING SAFETY

Even after the risks associated with a behavior or foodstuff is quantified, there remains the question of whether those risks are acceptable—that is, whether it is *safe*. *Safety*, as it is used in this context, refers to *acceptable risk*. The quantity of risk itself does not determine whether something is safe. For example, we might accept greater risk when eating raw sushi than when we are eating granola bars. In fact, differential acceptance of risk is common. We accept greater statistical risk of death when we drive than when we fly. We accept greater risk of injury when we play sports than when we walk to work. We accept greater risk of foodborne illness when we eat from street vendors than when we cook for ourselves at home.

The elimination of risk from food—a zero-risk diet—is not possible. It is tempting to think that, from an ethical perspective, we ought to try to reduce the health risk of foods as much as possible, to make things perfectly safe. However, it is clear from our behaviors that we do not actually believe this. A minimal-risk diet would involve not eating out, not eating raw and rare meats and fish, cooking all vegetables thoroughly, avoiding fresh fruits, and generally eating very highly processed, pasteurized, irradiated or preserved foods. This is not a diet that most people would choose—even if they knew that it would minimize food risk. Eating food is not only about getting calories and nutrition in as safe a way as possible. It is about aesthetics, experiences, convenience, sociability, cultural practice, and many other things as well. People are willing to trade these off against risk. People want fresh foods, diverse foods, exotic foods, and foods prepared by others.

How then should acceptable risk—safety—be determined? First, the goal cannot be that all foods, in all contexts, should have the same level of risk. The risks of restaurant-prepared raw fish sushi cannot be made the same as those of frozen dinners consumed at home. Safety must be food- and context-relative. What can be reasonably expected is that best safety practices are employed *for that food type and context*—e.g. sanitation facilities are provided in agricultural fields, animals are not fed meal from other slaughtered animals (which was the source of bovine spongiform encephalopathy (BSE) or mad cow disease), machinery is properly cleaned in processing facilities, food workers wear gloves and wash their hands regularly, sick animals are not incorporated into food products, possibly contaminated foods are pulled from supply chains, and so on. Determining what constitutes best practices in different forms of production, processing, transportation, retail, preparation and disposal will involve both scientific information and value judgments, since such things as capability and cost-effectiveness must be considered along with risk reduction.

Second, safety can and should be culturally sensitive, since people sometimes accept greater risks for cultural, aesthetic or historical reasons. An example of this mentioned earlier is that raw (unpasteurized) dairy consumption rates are much higher in parts of Europe than in the United States. Similarly, the bovine growth hormone (BGH) recombinant bovine somatotropin (rBST), which is given to cows to boost milk production, has been banned in the EU, Canada and New Zealand out of concerns for consumer health and animal welfare, yet it is widely used on dairy cattle in the United States. (In fact, any label in the United States that indicates that milk is BGH-free must include the disclaimer that the FDA finds no significant difference in milk from cows treated with growth hormones.) Because safety is *acceptable* risk, what threshold of risk counts as safe can be dependent upon social and cultural values.

Third, out of respect for individual autonomy, people should be permitted to take on significant risks if they choose to do so. People are allowed to voluntarily engage in enormously risky activities, even for merely recreational and peripheral reasons, so long as they are making adequately informed and non-coerced choices. People base jump, deep-sea dive, and eat puffer fish. What is crucial is that they are in a position to make those decisions, which requires being informed of known risks and possible hazards of foods—i.e. about the possible presence of allergens, pathogens, or chemical contaminants. (Of course, it also means being competent to make those decisions, which is why we protect children and other vulnerable people from their being exposed to unnecessary risks.)

HEALTH AND LABELING

The discussion above suggested that it is the responsibility of producers, supply chain actors and retailers to engage in best practices to reduce health risks and that it is the responsibility of regulators to help to ensure this. They should provide a basic level of safety, though they cannot be expected to accomplish perfect safety in all cases. Consumers can then take on higher- or lower-risk diets and, thereby, assume responsibility for their choices. However, there is a reasonable expectation that they will be informed about the significant risk-relevant features of foods prior to their choosing. This is typically done through informational labeling. (There are other possible principles for allocating responsibility. For example, on a *caveat emptor* or "buyer beware" principle, the consumer shoulders the responsibility for finding out about their purchases and assumes all the risks so long as the seller does not intentionally conceal known defects or provide false information about the product.)

As discussed in the previous chapter, decisions about what information goes on food labels are normative. It is not possible to put all the information about a product on its label (or on a menu). So, labeling is discriminatory; it involves prioritizing some information over other information. It involves choices that express value. It also places a burden—a cost and constraint—on the producer or retailer. In so doing, it signifies importance. We saw this in the discourse surrounding labeling for GMOs. The primary argument against labeling for GMOs is that it makes something not important, given substantial equivalence, seem important. This is also why the FDA requires the disclaimer on milk from cows given BGH.

Food labeling regulations in most countries have focused on food safety, health information, and honesty. In the United States, for example, early labeling regulations concerned not misleading consumers through false information about the product or unsubstantiated claims about its benefits. It has since expanded to providing positive information about ingredients and nutritional data, as well as information about potential risks, such as the presence of major allergens, the effects of alcohol on driving ability, and when the contents are hot. "Labeling" also occurs in restaurants through disclaimers on menus about the risks associated with particular foods or preparations, with signs and servers reminding patrons to provide information about their allergies, and with nutritional information about menu items. In some cases, these are required; in others, they are adopted as best practices for reasons to do with both consumer health and liability. Communication about health risks also takes the form of public advisories—e.g. regarding the presence of mercury in fish—and notifications when an outbreak occurs.

As the foregoing discussion illustrates, the trend in food labeling has been to provide consumers with more and more risk-relevant information. Again, the underlying normative principle is that people should be responsible for the risks associated with their food choices, so long as they are accurately, adequately and clearly informed about the foods they are buying—e.g. regarding allergens, ingredients, nutritional content and potential hazards. If consumers are not informed, they cannot be held responsible. However, due to the cost and space constraints associated with labels, there are also limitations on what can be reasonably expected—e.g. nutritional information cannot be provided for every age and body size. Thus, one normative dimension of health labeling (even after the principle above is accepted) is determining how comprehensive or specific the information included should be.

Another normative dimension of labeling relates to the need for consumers to understand the information on food labels, including its limitations, and to be able to interpret it for their own use. Studies have shown that consumer understanding of informational labels is quite low (Nielsen, 2012). What should be the role of producers, regulators and consumers in improving label comprehension? For example, do producers need to provide multilingual labels in some cases (or use symbols) or make nutritional information at restaurants more readily available? Do regulatory agencies need to improve public communication about the aims and limitations of labels? Is it up to consumers to be more proactive in learning about what labels do and do not tell them?

There is also a normative dimension to determining when information relevant to health and safety is sufficiently important and established that it should be required. How widespread does an allergy need to be before products containing the allergen should be positively labeled? How established does the science need to be before labels are altered to reflect new information about risk or nutrition—e.g. separating out different types of fat or carbohydrates? How should cases with high levels of uncertainty be treated—e.g. labeling for the presence of GMOs? Or for the possible presence of synthetic chemicals, the accumulation of which might lead to health problems? This issue arises as well with regard to honesty and misrepresentation. For example, at what percentage of filler or additives can a foodstuff no longer be called "meat," "natural," or "pure"?

Yet another normative issue is determining whether the informational requirements should be the same for all types of food products. For example, in the United States, claims about the health benefits of "conventional foods" are regulated more stringently than are claims about the health benefits of dietary supplements (e.g. vitamins and nutritional drinks). Is there a reasonable basis for differential standards in this and other cases?

What goes on a label, even for just health reasons (let alone for ecological or justice-related reasons), is contested because it involves protecting autonomy, promoting well-being, and allocating costs, benefits, burdens and responsibilities. It also involves making decisions about uncertainty and raises issues about paternalism and the appropriate role of government in our food systems. Even when there is fairly wide agreement on the operative normative principle, as there seems to be in this case, important normative issues arise in its application to concrete cases.

DEALING WITH UNCERTAINTY

The normative dimensions of decisions under uncertainty were addressed at length in the previous chapter (see, in particular, "Response to the innovation presumption: the precautionary principle"). It is not necessary to repeat that discussion here. Suffice it to say, the issue of how much precaution and how much confidence with which to proceed arises regarding novel processing techniques, additives, products and distribution systems (and other innovations), just as it does with novel agricultural technologies, such as GM crops. Moreover, as discussed above, judgments regarding risk, safety and labeling are never only quantitative, but are permeated with value judgments and commitments, even when they are not made explicit. It is for this reason that there is room for differential treatment of uncertainty and risk in different contexts and cases, and it is why an open and inclusive process for defining safety is crucial. Furthermore, as also already discussed, once determinations about risk management and safety are made, there are normative questions about allocating responsibilities and costs for accomplishing these, as well as about what strategies should be used—e.g. pre-market testing, post-market monitoring, market mechanisms, labeling, consumer advisories, and/or liability and litigation.

OBESITY AND PUBLIC HEALTH

The discussion above focused largely on discrete and communicable hazards, such as viruses and bacteria. However, many food health issues are more longitudinal. They are the result of widespread practices and behaviors accumulating over time. The case of chemical accumulation in the body—or "body burden"—is an instance of this. The obesity "epidemic" is another. *Overweight* and *obese* are defined in terms of weight-to-height ratio. (*Body Mass Index* (BMI) is mass divided by the square of height.) For example, the obesity cutoff point for a person 5'4" (1.63 m) is 174 lbs (79 Kg), and for a 5'9" person (1.75 m) it is 203 lbs (92 Kg) (Ogden et al., 2013). As mentioned earlier, there is a normative dimension to defining "overweight" and "obese," since it involves choosing what standards to use.

There has been a doubling of obesity rates globally since 1980. Nearly 1.5 billion adults (35%) are overweight, 500 million of whom (200 million men, 300 million women) are clinically obese. Some 170 million children under 18 are overweight or obese, and three quarters of the 40 million children under the age of five who are overweight live in developing countries (WHO, 2013; *The Lancet*, 2011). Thus, many developing countries now face what is being called the "double burden of malnutrition." They have widespread undernourishment (caloric and nutrient), as well as widespread overweight and obesity. They also sometimes face a third challenge associated with widespread foodborne and waterborne illnesses.

In many food-abundant nations, overweight and obesity levels are extraordinarily high. In the United States, 66% of adults are overweight (35% or 78 million of whom are obese) and 17% of children are obese (Ogden et al., 2012). In the UK, 26% of adults are obese (Swinburn et al., 2011; Wang et al., 2011). There is also a socio-economic dimension to the obesity crisis. In many places, low-income groups, minority groups, and women are disproportionately affected (DeSilver, 2013). For example, in the United States obesity rates are highest for Black (47.8%) and Hispanic (42.5%) adults.

Being overweight, and especially being obese, puts a person at higher risk for many noncommunicable diseases and/or conditions, such as heart disease, type 2 diabetes, high blood pressure, high cholesterol, stroke, some forms of cancer, and osteoarthritis. Obese individuals have medical costs 30% higher than those who are not overweight, and it is projected that in the United States 16% to 18% of medical expenditures will be associated with overweight and obesity by 2030 (Wang et al., 2011).

The causes of obesity are overconsumption of calorically dense and high-fat foods (i.e. high energy intake), as well as inadequate physical activity (i.e. low energy output). As discussed in Chapter 2, per capita caloric production has increased since the mid-twentieth century in all parts of the world, but particularly in many affluent regions. As a result, "cheap" calories are available, and they are used to sweeten processed foods and beverages, making them high in calories but low in nutrients. These are aggressively marketed, particularly to children. There have also been significant increases in portion sizes and snacking frequency. For example, in the United States, standard soft drink sizes have increased from 6.5 to 20 ounces since 1950, and per person consumption of sugary drinks is nearly 200 calories/day for men and over 100 calories/day for women. Among 12- to 19-year-olds, boys on average drink 22 ounces of full-calorie soda each day and girls drink 14.3 ounces each day (Ogden et al., 2011; CDC, 2011).

Globalization has helped to export these eating habits (e.g. snacking and fast food) and products (e.g. high-caloric drinks, processed foods and edible oils) around the world. As discussed in Chapter 1, a prominent concern regarding the global food system is the way in which it promotes and expands unhealthy diets, to which people are susceptible for cultural, economic, and psycho-physical reasons. These foods are calorie-dense and inexpensive; they are convenient; they are widely advertised; they are often associated with a higher quality of life; and we have an evolved proclivity for sweet and fatty high-caloric foods, since it was advantageous to pack calories during times of food availability in order to survive hunger seasons.

At the same time that calorie consumption has increased, energy expenditures have decreased. One of the primary reasons for this is urbanization. The majority of people now live in cities (or suburbs), and urban living is associated with lower levels of physical activity than is rural living. Increased rates of mechanized transportation— both automobiles and public transit—have also reduced physical activity, as has the expansion of more sedentary forms of work.

ACCESS TO HEALTHY FOODS

At the individual level, the causes of obesity are clear: increased caloric uptake and decreased caloric use resulting in *poor energy balance*. Therefore, addressing obesity involves improving people's diet and promoting regular physical activity. However, as alluded to above, there are structural factors that make these difficult—everything from where we live to the economics of food. To reduce obesity, people need to have access to healthier foods and opportunities for physical activity, and then they need to take advantage of them. There are thus two aspects to this problem: *availability* and *choice*.

Food availability was addressed at length in Chapter 2. The discussion there focused on undernutrition, but it applies as well to malnutrition associated with lack of access to healthy foods. For example, people who are food insecure are apt to purchase calorie-dense foods high in fat and sugar, rather than healthier, nutritionally rich foods, particularly when the former are less expensive and more readily available. Thus, one way to help to address the obesity crisis is to improve access to healthy foods by reducing poverty, making them less expensive, expanding their production, and improving their distribution. As in the case of undernutrition, these are impacted by a wide variety of public policies, such as assistance programs, agricultural subsidies, commerce regulations, and labor laws, as well as by broader features of food systems. One of the arguments for alternative food systems is that they provide healthier foods than does the global food system.

Public policies and programs also impact opportunities for physical activity. For example, transportation policies and urban design affect people's ability to walk to work, school and services. Policing and neighborhood security programs can be important for providing safe public spaces for sports. Educational policies are relevant to whether the school day includes time for gym and recess.

As with malnutrition, there are many potential win-wins when addressing the factors that give rise to a lack of access to nutritional foods and opportunities for physical activity. For example, better diet and exercise are associated with improved school performance. Reducing poverty increases the welfare of those who were poor and has substantial social benefits (e.g. increased economic activity and civic involvement). Walkable communities and safe public spaces foster social capital and recreational opportunities. Thus, it is possible to address the *access* dimension to obesity, and thereby dramatically improve public health, in ways that are widely regarded as not only acceptable, but in many cases also ethically good or perhaps even required for reasons related to social justice.

RESPONSIBILITY AND CHOICE

One of the primary ethical issues regarding the choice dimension of the obesity crisis concerns whose responsibility it is to address it. The global industrial food system excels at delivering what people want, when they want it, at a price they are willing to pay. That it does so well satisfying people's food preferences is one of the primary arguments for the system. Therefore, one prominent view is that, in places where there is access to healthy foods and physical exercise, obesity is primarily a matter of personal responsibility. It is up to individuals (and, in the case of children, their parents) to change their eating habits. The global food system just delivers whatever people want, as indicated by what they buy and how much they are willing to pay for it; and what people want are foods that are high in fat, sugar and sodium. If people wanted healthier foods, that is what the system would deliver.

In response to this, critics often point out that the corporations that sell unhealthy foods are not merely satisfying people's preferences. They try to shape people's preferences. Their goal—and their fiduciary obligation in many cases—is not to promote public health, or even public welfare, but to maximize profits. Their primary products are highly processed, high-caloric foods, and this is where they generate most of their revenue. Many of these companies do not also sell fresh foods; or, if they do, they cannot do so as profitably or as widely and easily. Therefore, they have a strong interest in maintaining and growing public consumption of unhealthy foods. They are aided in this by the fact that humans have a predilection for sugary, fatty, and high-sodium foods and beverages. But they also actively promote public demand. One way this is done is by lobbying for commerce, labor and agricultural policies that keep the cost of processed foods low in comparison to healthier foods. Another way is by making them widely and easily available through such things as franchise proliferation, globalization and vending machines. A third way is by advertising them.

Marketing and promotion of unhealthy foods far outstrips that of healthy foods. In the United States, fast food companies spent $4.6 billion USD on advertising in 2012, and the food and beverage industry as a whole spent well over $10 billion USD. That same year, only $116 million USD was spent advertising fruits and vegetables in the United States—McDonald's alone spent over two-and-a-half times that amount. Globally, the Coca-Cola Company spent nearly $3 billion USD on advertising in 2012. A great deal of this advertising was aimed at children. In the United States, children aged 2 to 11 years old see approximately 13 food and beverage advertisements on television per day, while 12- to 17-year-olds see approximately 16 per day. The vast majority of these—84% in 2009—are for unhealthy foods. In fact, on children's programming, 95% of the food and beverage advertisements were for products high in fat, sugar and sodium (Powell et al., 2013). Advertisements aimed at children often use cartoon and other characters that appeal to them and often highlight the toys and games that come with the food. It is effective. Exposure is correlated with children being more apt to ask their parents for the products, as well as with increased consumption of them. In Quebec, where electronic and print fast food advertising aimed at children has been prohibited for decades, child obesity rates are well below those for Canada as a whole (Dhar and Baylis, 2011).

Many people consider unhealthy food advertising targeted to children to be unethical. The reason for this is that its goal is to manipulate children into doing things that are bad for them in order to make a profit. There is no doubt that diets high in fat, sugar and sodium are unhealthy for kids, both immediately and in the long term. Overweight and obesity increase the risk for both childhood and adult diseases and disorders, including diabetes, heart disease, asthma and depression. There is also no doubt that targeting advertising to children is done in order to make a profit. The reason that it is thought to be exploitative or manipulative is that young children do not understand that commercials are intended to be persuasive, that they are selling something. In fact, children under the age of six do not even distinguish between programming and advertisements. Therefore, advertisers are taking advantage of children's vulnerability—their inability to think critically about what they are seeing—to get them to form preferences and habits that are lasting and detrimental to their well-being. It is not all that different from using cartoon characters and placing advertisements in children's line of sight to make cigarettes attractive to them.

In response to this argument, it is often pointed out that young children do not purchase their food; their parents do. Moreover, parents are responsible for their children's exposure to advertisements. The reason that children see so many is because they have so much screen time. In the United States, children on average watch approximately 3 hours of television per day and have approximately 5 to 7 hours of screen time. Parents buy their children cell phones, permit them to have televisions and computers in their bedrooms, and allow them to spend hours playing video games. In fact, children's viewing habits, like their eating habits, track those of their parents. The more television their parents watch, the more they watch. The more fast food their parents eat, the more they eat. The less their parents exercise, the less they exercise. Therefore, it is the responsibility of parents to model better lifestyles, monitor their children's exposure to advertising (as well as explain to them what advertisements are), and purchase healthier foods.

There is certainly merit to the view that parents shoulder a great deal of responsibility for the diets and physical activities of their children. But, as has been highlighted several times, people's food choices are structured by such things as cost, taste, availability, social norms and convenience. Right now, these factors favor unhealthy choices. Moreover, children often have opportunities to get unhealthy foods outside of their parents' supervision—e.g. from vending machines or through school lunches. So, while it is undoubtedly true that parents are responsible for the health and well-being of their children and that this extends to diet and exercise, it does not follow that they are solely responsible.

If we understand "responsibility" in terms of what is required to address the problem, rather than who is blameworthy for bringing it about, it is clear that parents alone are not responsible. This public health challenge is so widespread, severe and systematic that consumers, parents, producers, educators, health professionals and governments are all needed in order to meet it. Parents need to model and promote good eating habits and exercise, as well as reduce their children's screen time (which involves both exposure to advertisements and sedentariness). Producers need to provide healthier food options and better (and more accessible) nutritional information about their products, as well refrain from promoting unhealthy eating to kids. Schools need to provide healthy lunches and opportunities for physical activity, as well as educate students about the importance of diet and exercise. Health care systems need to emphasize the importance of a healthy diet and exercise, and encourage people to engage in these through such things as nutritional counseling and subsidizing the costs of exercise. Government and civic organizations need to develop and disseminate dietary guidelines, reduce the cost of healthy foods, foster expansion of their distribution, refrain from subsidizing (directly or indirectly) unhealthy foods, and plan walkable urban environments. This is not meant to be an exhaustive list of prescriptions, but a representative sample of possibilities. Since the problem is both individual and systematic, the solution needs to be so as well.

REGULATION AND PUBLIC HEALTH

An ethical issue that has become prominent in the context of addressing the obesity crisis, particularly in the United States, is the use of governmental power to promote public health. It is widely agreed that governments have a vital role to play in addressing overweight and obesity. The issue is what methods of doing so are appropriate. Should their activities be primarily educational and informational—e.g. dietary guidelines and informational labeling? Should they attempt to "nudge" people toward better choices with persuasion and programs—e.g. public service announcements and health classes in schools? Should they intervene in the marketplace—e.g. by taxing unhealthy foods, subsidizing healthy ones, and restricting advertising toward children? Should they prohibit certain types of foods altogether—e.g. those containing synthetic trans fats or supersized sugary drinks?

The last of these—restrictive regulation—is particularly controversial because it involves limiting people's options. For example, an attempted ban on high-caloric beverages above 16 ounces in New York City was widely opposed, and subsequently judged by the courts to be illegal, on the grounds that it went beyond the authority of the Board of Health that instituted it. As discussed earlier, consideration of autonomy generally favors allowing people to engage in risky behaviors, so long as they choose to do so and are not coerced. Given this presumption, there needs to be good reasons for why government has an interest—or standing—to intervene. One commonly recognized justification is that the state can intervene when a behavior poses risks to others. For example, the basis for prohibiting cigarette-smoking in many public places is that secondhand smoke is unhealthy for others. However, many people argue, food is not like this. If a person chooses to eat foods that are high in fat, sugar and sodium, it does not increase the risk of heart disease for anyone else. Thus, there does not seem to be a public protection justification for the state to promote healthy eating in ways that restrict people's food choices or that make it more difficult (or costly) for them to act on their food preferences. On this view, coercive food policies are unjustifiably paternalistic.

One response to this view is that it does not hold with respect to children. The state has a responsibility to protect their health and welfare. Therefore, school lunches and food subsidies aimed at children can and should promote healthy eating. Another response is that the state has a strong interest in reducing risky behaviors when it shoulders a significant portion of the associated medical costs. This justification has been used in support of mandatory seat belt and helmet laws, for example. As mentioned earlier, in the United States it is projected that 16% to 18% of medical costs will be associated with obesity by 2030, and over a quarter of Americans have a government-based health plan—Medicare, Medicaid or military/veterans' benefits (Mendes, 2012). Already, obesity-related illness constitutes 9% of Medicare spending. In the UK and Canada, where there are single-payer health care systems, nearly all obesity-related health care costs are shouldered by taxpayers. A third response is that concerns about state intervention to promote public health are based on a restrictive conception of the appropriate role of government. If government ought to not only protect its citizens from harm, but also promote their well-being, then perhaps aggressive anti-obesity measures are justified on the same grounds as are publicly funded education, scientific research, and infrastructure.

Public policies can improve people's diets. Bans on synthetic trans fats in some cities in the United States have dramatically decreased their use throughout the country, and the FDA is now considering a national ban. Research has shown that a tax on unhealthy foods to internalize their social costs reduces their consumption. Subsidies for and removal of taxes and tariffs on fresh produce can increase their consumption. Agricultural policies that promote nutritional foods over caloric quantity can improve the healthfulness of the food supply overall. The normative question is not whether these sorts of interventions work. Rather, it is whether they fall within the appropriate scope of government or whether, instead, they inappropriately restrict people's choices or favor particular conceptions of how people should live.

NUTRITIONISM, DIETARY SUPPLEMENTS AND DIETING

Several of the topics discussed in this and previous chapters concern the nutritional content of people's diets. *Nutritionism* refers to conceptions of good food and good diet that focus on nutritional composition, rather than foods, dietary practices and lifestyles. On a nutritionist outlook, healthy eating involves optimizing the calories, vitamins, amino acids and other inputs in our body. Nutritionism is expressed through such things as labeling policies and nutritional guidelines oriented around the daily intake of nutrients, diets that focus on restricting or promoting particular nutritional components, micronutrient fortification of foods, and expansion of the dietary supplement industry—half of Americans and a third of Britons now take daily supplements.

Many people believe that nutritionism is both an increasingly common way to think about food and a problematic one. One concern about nutritionism is that it actually leads people to make poor food evaluations and choices. For example, it results in certain foods being avoided, such as eggs and butter, when they can be part of a healthy diet. It leads people to adopt fad diets that focus on particular nutrients, such as high-protein and no-carb diets, which are difficult to sustain and can be unhealthy. It causes people to believe that all calories and nutrients are substitutable, when not all ways of getting them are equal with respect to how they are used by the body. It leads people to be susceptible to overhyped claims about supplements and services, and to spend billions of dollars on them, even though they do not improve people's health.

Another concern about nutritionism is that it is a techno-scientific way of approaching food that mistakenly favors an engineering approach to addressing our health challenges. On this view, nutritional inadequacy is a symptom of problematic food production systems and dietary practices. Therefore, it needs to be addressed as part of reforms to those systems and to our lifestyles, rather than by engineering nutrition into otherwise unhealthy foods or supplementing our otherwise unhealthy (or inadequate) diets with pills and powders. Dieting, supplements and fortification are technofixes that do not address the cause of the problem, which is an industrial food system that produces inexpensive, calorie-dense and nutrient-poor convenience foods. Nutritionism, rather than being an antidote to this system, is part and parcel of it. It is a false trope—we can keep the system and still get the nutrients we need. The alternative to nutritionism's reductionist understanding of food and health problems is one that appreciates the ecological, economic, social and cultural factors that give rise to nutritionally poor diets and that aims to address them. Moreover, a "good diet" is not only a nutritionally adequate one. The cultural, social and aesthetic dimensions of food belie the view that food is just fuel.

The concerns about nutritionism raised above include both general cultural critiques and criticisms of modern food science and nutrient-oriented food policies and practices. One response to them is that they are too broad. They lump together nutritional sciences and nutritionists with fad diets and corporate marketing. It may be true that the benefits of many nutritional supplements are overstated, that fortification is an inadequate response to nutrient-poor diets, and that single-dimension diets do not promote healthy lifestyles. But it does not follow from this that studying and educating people about the nutritional dimensions of the foods that they eat is problematic. In fact, the nutritionism critique seems to commit the *false dilemma fallacy*. There is no reason that a nutrient-level understanding of food cannot be part of a more comprehensive approach to addressing malnourishment and undernourishment.

Another response is that if people are going to eat unhealthy diets—which they seem to want to do—it is better that they nutritionally supplement them than that they do not. Moreover, nutrient-level information about the foods that they eat can help to move people toward healthier diets. The nutritionism critique seems to assume that food science and nutritional enhancement are enablers of unhealthy diets and industrial food systems. However, even if this is true within large food corporations and the nutritional supplements industry, it is not true of nutrition scientists and practitioners generally, many of whom are dedicated to improving people's diets and lifestyles. It is also sometimes pointed out that nutritionism is a food abundance issue. For those who are malnourished from lack of access to adequate nutrition, micronutrient supplements are vital.

Critics of nutritionism might acknowledge that food science and a focus on the nutritional components of food are not opposed to systematic reform of food systems and practices in theory, but argue that they undermine reform in practice by promising an alternative route to a healthy diet and by distracting attention away from the systemic problems. Food news and education become about diets, dietary guidelines and particular nutrients and supplements. Moreover, nutritionism plays into the strengths of food and beverage marketing. Food companies can promote the nutritionally enhanced aspects of their foods and make them appear healthy, when they are not.

EATING DISORDERS

Eating disorders are abnormal behaviors involving food that result in insufficient or excessive food intake to the detriment of a person's health, often accompanied by extreme stress and concern about body shape or weight. The three most common eating disorders are anorexia nervosa, bulimia nervosa and binge eating. Anorexia is when individuals believe they are overweight, even when they are extremely underweight, and severely restrict their food intake as a result. Bulimia is when individuals eat excessive amounts of food and then purge themselves of it through vomiting, laxative use, and/or extreme dieting. Binge eating is when individuals eat large amounts of food in short periods of time while feeling a lack of control. Eating disorders are widespread. It is estimated that approximately 2.5% of people in the UK and approximately 4% of people in the United States suffer from them at some point in their lives, the vast majority of whom are women (NIMH, 2014; Beat, 2010).

Eating disorders are complex psycho-bio-social problems. They are addressed through therapy, education, family counseling, medicine, and, in some cases, hospitalization and monitoring. Ethical issues arise regarding both their causes and their treatment. Regarding their causes, concerns are commonly raised about the role that cultural "ideals" of beauty play in them. Advertising, entertainment, fashion and popular culture generally associate thinness with attractiveness and sexiness. This generates significant social pressure to have the "right" type of body and to control one's weight, which can lead to anxiety and foster abnormal behavior around eating. As a result, there is thought to be a shared social responsibility to address this contributing cause of eating disorders. It is also part of why placing full responsibility on those who suffer from eating disorders—for their lack of self-control or weakness—is considered an instance of blaming the victim.

With respect to treatment, eating disorders raise a number of ethical issues associated with medical decision-making. Standard informed consent models of medical decision-making prioritize patient autonomy. People do not need to undergo treatment if they do not want to do so. However, medical professionals and proxies should also be guided by beneficence, particularly if a person is not able to provide informed consent. Extreme cases of eating disorders therefore raise the question of whether, and under what conditions, it is justified to treat a person against her will. If a person with anorexia needs life-saving treatment, is it permissible to do so even if she does not want it? What if the person's life is not at risk, but she is terribly unhealthy? How does this differ for adults and minors? This issue is complicated by the psychological component of eating disorders—e.g. should refusal of treatment in extreme cases be construed as an indication of lack of competence to make medical decisions (as it is sometimes with addiction)? It is also complicated by the fact that a contributing cause to eating disorders frequently is a feeling of lack of control and disempowerment in other aspects of life.

The tension between a duty of beneficence and respect for autonomy also arises regarding particular treatments—for example, invasive monitoring (e.g. in bathrooms) and restricting activities (e.g. hospitalization). Is "threat to self" applicable in the case of eating disorders, as it is when people are judged to be a suicide risk? Or is this a case more like extreme rock-climbing and base-jumping, in which coercive (as opposed to persuasive) interventions are not accepted out of respect for autonomy, even when there is a very high risk of injury and mortality.

As with most medical and psychological disorders, the ethical questions around eating disorders are not to do with whether they are good or bad, but with how they are defined, diagnosed and treated; the allocation of responsibilities and resources to prevent and address them; and how to make decisions in difficult cases, such as when autonomy and beneficence appear to be in tension or when informed consent is not obtainable.

CONCLUSION

It is widely agreed that everyone ought to have access to a safe and healthy diet. However, what counts as "safe," "healthy" and "access" are contested. So too is whose responsibility it is to provide these and when and how it is appropriate for our state, our friends and our family to step in to help us make safer and healthier food decisions. The goal of this chapter has been to elucidate the range of normative issues related to food and health, and the values and principles that are operative in them, with a particular focus on foodborne illness (food safety) and obesity (public health). As with almost all food issues, these are bound up in the discourse surrounding food systems, food technologies, food policies and food choices. Moreover, as the section on eating disorders indicates, they are only part of the ethical landscape around health and food. Food is crucial to our well-being, but it is also a source of stress, anxiety and hazard.

FURTHER READING

Several of the books on food systems and food ethics listed at the end of Chapter 1 address issues related to agriculture, food and health. Eric Schlosser's *Fast Food Nation* (Houghton Mifflin) has been particularly influential. Books specifically on the social, political and/or ethical dimensions of food and health issues include:

Marion Nestle, *Safe Food: The Politics of Food Safety* (University of California Press)

Marion Nestle, *Food Politics: How the Food Industry Influences Nutrition and Health* (University of California Press)

Jeff Benedict, *Poisoned: The True Story of the Deadly E. Coli Outbreak that Changed the Way Americans Eat* (Inspire Books)

Janet Poppendieck, *Free for All: Fixing School Food in America* (University of California Press)

Michael Pollan, *In Defense of Food: An Eater's Manifesto* (Penguin)

Gyorgy Scrinis, *Nutritionism: The Science and Politics of Dietary Advice* (Columbia University Press)

Julie Guthman, *Weighing In: Obesity, Food Justice, and the Limits of Capitalism* (University of California Press)

Alexandra Brewis, *Obesity: Cultural and Biocultural Perspectives* (Rutgers University Press)

FOOD AND CULTURE

We are cultural animals. The distinctive features of our form of life—our way of going about the world—are our complex belief systems, social arrangements and technologies. Other species use tools, engage in social learning, and have social organization. However, no species innovates, accumulates or disseminates these on anything approaching the rate and scale that we do. The reason for this is that we have cognitive and psychological capacities, beyond those of individuals of other species, which enable us to imagine ways the world might be different, devise strategies to bring them about, and then disseminate our knowledge and innovations to others.

That rationality, learning and innovation are central to how we live is the source of cultural diversity. Different populations of people developed distinctive belief systems, technologies and practices over time, particularly when they had limited exchange (e.g. trade and migration) with other peoples. One respect in which peoples diverged is in their *foodways*–what foods they eat, how they produce (or acquire) them, how they prepare them (and who does the preparing), how they consume them (and with whom they do so), and their traditions and rituals around them. A significant part of the explanation for cultural divergence in foodways is ecological. People on Pacific islands had access to different resources, experienced different climates, and faced different ecological challenges and opportunities than did people in the Fertile Crescent or in the Arctic, for example. As a result, they developed different foodways and cultural practices, worldviews and narratives involving them. Cultural identities, meanings and norms are therefore embedded in and expressed through food in much the same way that they are in language.

As discussed in the Introduction, this book is not a study or review of particular foodways. However, the fact that food and culture are so tightly connected, and the fact that culture is crucial to identity and meaning in our lives, gives rise to a number of ethical issues. This chapter focuses on ethical issues at the intersection of food and culture.

RESPECTING CULTURE

Cultural identity refers to a person's recognition of a culture as her own. Most of us identify with one or more cultures—ethnic, religious or national/regional, for example. Cultural situatedness and identity provide sense of place, meaning and orientation in the world, while also strengthening social connections. It can be vital to individual well-being and flourishing. Several studies have shown that strong cultural identity contributes positively to people's happiness. This is the *value of culture*. Culture can also create value. Places, practices, objects and interactions become valuable when they play a role in a culture's stories, narratives, social structures, worldviews and rituals. This is *cultural value*. Concerns about respect for cultural identity and cultural value often arise in the context of agriculture and food. I have already discussed several instances of this at some length, so will only briefly review them here.

INSENSITIVITY TO DIFFERENCE

As alluded to in the context of the GMO labeling and obesity discussions, government ought to be neutral with respect to cultures and worldviews. The state should not aim to promote one over the others, especially when its citizens are culturally diverse. Therefore, food policies should not presume one culture or religion. For example, if there are not religiously appropriate foods in school lunch programs, then students may have to choose between eating and being faithful to their values/traditions. Similarly, social events, both public and private, at which culturally appropriate foods are not available may unintentionally exclude or marginalize people. Thus, one issue to do with respect for cultural difference is the extent to which institutions and individuals have an obligation to provide for cultural differences around food, as well as the extent to which expectations must be reasonably circumscribed by cost and availability.

Inadequate recognition of cultural diversity in food policies and practices is often the result of cultural myopia or a lack of appreciation that there are cultural perspectives other than one's own and that things may look very different from them. For example, it may be that from some perspectives the only reasonable concerns about GM crops are their health risks, so that if they are shown to be safe, then labeling is unjustified. However, there are other perspectives on which gene-level engineering is considered intrinsically problematic. Positive labeling would help people who embrace such worldviews to eat in accordance with their value commitments. Similarly, the Makah whale hunt may look problematic from an ecological and animal welfare perspective, and it may seem to not even be a traditional cultural practice, since it uses modern technologies. Yet, from the perspective of those participating in it, it has enormous cultural value—it promotes cultural identity and fosters cultural pride. Therefore, a crucial step toward respecting cultural differences around foods is trying to understand food issues from the cultural perspectives (and not just the economic or the health perspectives) of those involved.

INJUSTICE AND EXPLOITATION

Food and agricultural policies can have differential cultural impacts, often in ways that are detrimental to those who are already disadvantaged or marginalized. This is thought to be the case, for instance, with national and international policies and trade agreements that promote commodity monoculture and displace traditional smallholding agriculture. For example, Vandana Shiva has described the cascading effects that consolidated land ownership and power over the seed supply can have on small-scale producers, agricultural communities, and associated cultural practices. She emphasizes the ways in which agricultural festivals, rituals and practices—such as those around sharing seeds—are central to relationships and social systems in many smallholding communities.

Policies that favor commodity monoculture and industrial food systems can also make traditional foods and preparations more difficult to maintain. For instance, Shiva highlights how policies restricting small-scale mustard seed oil production in India were not only economically disadvantageous to the poor (both producers and consumers), but also promoted a shift to soy oil, which is culturally inappropriate and controlled by large (often global) actors rather than by local producers. Natural resource management policies can also have differential cultural impacts. For example, water management policies for rivers in the Pacific Northwest of the United States affect salmon runs that are economically and culturally central to Native American groups in the area. More water diverted to agriculture means less for the salmon and those who depend upon them.

Injustice is also thought to occur when cultural knowledge is used without appropriate consent or compensation, or when it is done in ways that are contrary to the culture's worldviews. This is the concern behind *biopiracy*—i.e. exploitative use of local or indigenous biological knowledge to create commercialized products. *Bioprospecting*, exploring for biological resources that could be developed into new products, is common in the agricultural and pharmaceutical industries, and it very often draws upon indigenous knowledge of plants and animals. Bioprospecting has been, and continues to be, a fruitful source of biotechnological innovation. However, because it makes use of cultural knowledge, it must be done in ways that are fair and culturally sensitive. When it is not—when it is done without consent of the communities, does not benefit the communities, or involves culturally offensive practices—then it is regarded as unjust. For example, several Ojibway tribes in North America have objected to the genetic modification and patenting of traditionally cultivated varieties of wild rice on the grounds that it will economically disadvantage them (by competing with their wild rice production, contaminating their rice beds, and opening them to patent infringement liability) and that genetic modification and patenting are contrary to their cultural practices and worldviews regarding the integrity of wild rice, common heritage, and ownership.

HOMOGENIZATION AND LOSS

As discussed in Chapter 1, a prominent concern regarding the global industrial food system is that it promotes standardization in production processes and products, thereby decreasing cultural diversity and displacing traditional agricultural and culinary practices. The widespread presence of fast food franchises is symbolic of this homogenization (sometimes called "Americanization"). There are now over 32,000 McDonald's restaurants in 117 countries. However, it is also evident in the growth of commodity monoculture, the dramatic reduction in the varieties of crops and animals cultivated, the shift from smallholding landownership to large-scale and corporate ownership, and the enormous increases in the consumption of processed foods and beverages globally.

Standardized production and convenience foods are thought to undermine not only cultural diversity in food and agriculture, but also their meaning and value in our lives. The rise of inexpensive convenience foods is correlated with less time spent on food preparation and eating with friends and family. One worry associated with this is that culinary knowledge and skills are not being passed on—i.e. culturally valuable practices and opportunities are being lost in much the same way that heritage is lost when languages are not learned by the next generation. Another worry is that food is losing its power as the locus around which families are brought together and cultural identities expressed. Yet another worry is that this is contributing to a loss of food aesthetics and appreciation. The concern is that people increasingly think of food as fuel or in terms of its nutritional content, and are satisfied with mass-manufactured processed food products. As discussed in Chapter 1, these are precisely the types of concerns that animate the slow food and local food movements.

Worries about cultural loss and homogenization give rise to a number of food policy issues. For example, to what extent can trade policies, regulations and subsidies be justified on the grounds that they protect traditional forms of agriculture that are culturally valued and connected to cultural identity? What is the role of government in promoting and maintaining culturally significant culinary practices? And what means of doing so are acceptable—e.g. education, incentives or subsidies? These questions intersect with many of the considerations that arose in the discussion on the state's role in promoting public health (Chapter 5), such as the appropriate use of state power and resources, paternalism, and individual autonomy. If people want to eat inexpensive fast and processed foods produced by global corporations, does the value of cultural tradition and history provide a basis for intervening in the marketplace and expending state resources to protect them?

PROBLEMATIC CULTURAL PRACTICES

The discussion above highlighted food issues that arise from a lack of respect for culture, diversity and difference. However, cultural practices around food can themselves be problematic.

In some cases, culturally valued practices are ecologically problematic. For example, traditions in China and other countries in Asia regarding the symbolic and medicinal power of shark fin soup is driving the practice of capturing sharks only for their fins and discarding the rest of their body. Finning, along with other forms of commercial fishing and the impacts of by-catch, is having a devastating effect on shark populations, particularly given their comparatively slow reproductive rates. Tens of millions of sharks are killed each year, and according to the International Union for the Conservation of Nature, which conducts biodiversity assessments and maintains the Red List of threatened species, a quarter of ray and shark species are threatened with extinction (IUCN, 2014). Moreover, because sharks are large predators, the reduction in their numbers has cascading effects throughout aquatic food webs and systems. The practice of eating shark fin soup was not ecologically problematic when human populations were smaller, there was less capacity to capture, preserve and transport the animals, and it was not accessible to most people for social and economic reasons. However, industrialized fishing, global distribution systems, economic development, and social change have contributed to its becoming so. Shark fin soup is not a unique case. The situation is similar with respect to traditions and beliefs regarding the medicinal use and consumption of parts of gorillas, rhinos, tigers, and many reptile species, as well as with many commercially harvested and hunted species, such as bluefin tuna, glass eels, and numerous migratory bird species.

The foregoing are examples of culturally significant food practices and traditions that contribute to ecological and biodiversity problems. Again, the cultural traditions or practices are not themselves regarded as problematic, but have become so in the context of a global industrial food system, where there are not adequate controls, regulations, and best practices to conserve resources and protect species. However, there are other cultural practices around food and agriculture that are regarded as problematic in themselves. Some of these involve nonhuman animals—e.g. drive-hunting dolphins and force-feeding fowl for foie gras. But many concern gender roles and expectations. Food preparation responsibilities fall disproportionately on women. In many cultural traditions, women's primary role is thought to be homemaker and foodmaker. In some cases, men eat first, more, and/or nutritionally superior foods. Women in many cultures are expected to strictly monitor food intake to maintain particular body types and appearances so as to be attractive to men. Women and girls disproportionately suffer from eating disorders. The examples could go on, but in each case the cultural practices are thought to be problematic because they both express and perpetuate problematic power relationships, norms, roles and expectations.

One area where expression of gender norms and expectations has gotten considerable attention in recent years is in food advertising. Products associated with food preparation are targeted largely to women and often exploit the expectation that good women (in addition to being thin) keep an immaculate home in which their family is well fed. Feminine "ideals" regarding weight and body type are leveraged, and so propagated, to sell diet systems, yogurt and breakfast cereals. In food advertisements aimed at men—e.g. beer and restaurant commercials aired during sporting events—women are routinely objectified, over-sexualized, poorly treated, or ridiculed (portrayed as materialistic, dumb, overly emotional, or nagging, for example). Manliness is associated with eating meat and lots of it—big burgers and buckets of chicken wings—and effeminate men are mocked (and in some cases even hit). Even when commercials intentionally exaggerate gendered stereotypes, expectations and roles around food to poke fun at them, which is increasingly common, they are operative. In some cases, they are overt and explicit even in names—e.g. Hooters Restaurants, Skinny

Girl Vodka and Manwich sloppy joe sauce. Misrepresentation, biased representation, stereotypical representation, and offensive representation in food advertisements are of course not limited to sex and gender. It occurs with race, ethnicity, sexual orientation and class as well.

ETHICAL RELATIVISM

Because cultural practices can sometimes be problematic, an important issue in food ethics is how much normative significance cultural considerations should be afforded. Can the fact that something is part of a cultural tradition make it acceptable if it would otherwise be considered ethically objectionable? This question concerns the justificatory power of appeals to cultural practices and traditions.

When considering the normativity of cultural practices, it is important to keep in mind the distinction between *justification* and *explanation*. That there is an explanation for how things came to be leaves open the question of whether things *ought* to be that way. To see this, consider an obvious case. The explanation for why a man abuses his wife might appeal to his childhood experiences, his lack of emotional control, his economic situation, his substance abuse, or his perceptions of her behavior. But the existence of such explanations does not justify the action as acceptable or as something that ought to continue; spousal abuse is clearly unethical, even if we can explain why it occurs. There is an explanation for all cultural practices—i.e. an account of the historical, economic, ecological and social factors that caused it to come about. However, it does not follow from this that all cultural practices are justified in the sense that there are good reasons for their continuation. For example, over the course of human history, many cultures have practiced slavery. In each case, there is an explanation for how the practice came about. However, the fact that it was economically expedient or sanctioned by religious authority does not justify it as ethically acceptable. (The issue here is not whether people in that cultural context would endorse it, but whether or not it should have been done.) It is not always valid to infer from the fact that something is a cultural practice or tradition to the conclusion that it is ethically acceptable to engage in that practice. In Chapter 3,

I referred to this as the *fallacy of appeal to tradition*. (It is also important to keep in mind the distinction between evaluating a practice and ascribing praise or blame. We might judge a person who owned slaves when the practice was legal and widely accepted less harshly than we do a person who engages in illegal human trafficking today. But this should not be conflated with the idea that slavery today is ethically worse than slavery throughout history. Justification needs to be distinguished from culpability, just as it must be from explanation.)

Some people claim to believe that all of ethics is relative to culture. That is, they endorse a view regarding the grounding of ethical truth called *cultural relativism*. (The field of study that concerns the nature of ethics is called *metaethics*; so, cultural relativism is a theory or view in metaethics.) According to cultural relativism, the truth value of claims about what is ethically right and wrong, or good and bad, is determined by cultural norms and practices. That is to say, an action or practice is wrong if it is contrary to what one's culture does, and an action or practice is right if it conforms to cultural norms. For example, according to cultural relativism, whether it is ethically acceptable to eat foie gras depends upon whether eating foie gras is part of one's cultural practices. If it is widely accepted and historically done, then it is ethically acceptable to do it. If it is widely objected to and there are laws against it, then it is ethically wrong. Again, according to cultural relativism, ethics is determined by cultural practices and norms. There is no fallacy of appeal to tradition.

The most prominent objection to cultural relativism is that it has highly counterintuitive implications. If what is right and wrong is relative to a culture and a culture endorses child sacrifice, selling women as if they are property, or genocide against a minority group, then these are ethically right to do for people in that culture. Moreover, no cultural practices are ethically better or worse than any other; they are all ethically right (because they determine what is ethically right) within that culture. In addition, cultures never improve ethically, they just change. According to cultural relativism, it was right for women to not be able to own property or to vote in the United States and England, and for people of color to be enslaved, when that was the prevailing sentiment and law of the land. So nothing got ethically better when those sentiments, practices and laws changed. (Another set of difficulties regarding cultural relativism concerns defining what constitutes a distinct culture and, if that can be done, what determines the norms for the culture—e.g. laws, ideals or actual practices.)

Once people who claim to endorse cultural relativism understand the implications of the view—i.e. that it could be ethically right to systematically discriminate against, enslave and kill innocent people—they very often revise their view to what might be called *selective relativism*. According to selective relativism, some ethical claims are culturally relative, but not all are. (I discuss selective relativism below.) However, some continue to endorse cultural relativism. But if cultural relativism has strongly counterintuitive implications, then a strong argument must be provided for accepting it. What is the argument for cultural relativism?

The core argument for cultural relativism is the *argument from cultural divergence*. The argument begins with the observation that different cultures have different ethical beliefs and embrace different practices and norms. Some cultures have a caste system, others do not. Some afford women the same legal rights and protections as men, others do not. Some use corporeal punishment and the death penalty in their criminal justice systems, others do not. Some allow the hunting of dolphins, others do not. The argument then continues by claiming that there is no standard outside of some cultural perspective by which to evaluate different cultural practices, norms and beliefs. Because all evaluations must assume some cultural perspective, they are also culturally relative. Thus, not only are all ethical claims and norms part of some cultural perspective, so too are all evaluations of them. There is simply no getting beyond or outside of culture when it comes to either making or evaluating ethical claims.

The core component of the argument from cultural divergence is sometimes called the *challenge of adjudication*. If cultural relativism is false, then it must be possible to evaluate the ethical beliefs and norms of a culture as more or less justified, and this requires that there be a culturally independent standard for evaluation. That is, there must be some method for adjudicating among different cultures' ethical beliefs and practices which does not itself assume some culture's particular ethical beliefs and norms (otherwise, it would *beg the question*). This, after all, is how cross-cultural empirical disagreements are settled. There is a standard, independent of any particular culture, which can adjudicate across cultures—i.e. the scientific method. We do not think that the truth regarding claims about the shape of the earth, the relationship between mass and gravity, or the existence of dinosaurs are culturally relative, because there is an effective method of evaluation and adjudication for empirical claims. The argument from cultural divergence claims that there is no such standard or method for ethical beliefs.

Responding to the challenge of adjudication and the argument from cultural divergence requires demonstrating that there are nonrelativistic ways to evaluate ethical claims and beliefs. Many people believe that there are. In fact, several of them have been discussed throughout this book. One way it is possible to evaluate ethical claims is by assessing empirical assumptions used to support them. For example, as discussed in Chapter 3, one of the considerations offered in support of the ethical acceptability of eating animals was that they do not feel pain. However, there is strong physiological and behavioral evidence that they do feel pain. Therefore, that is an unsound justification for the ethical acceptability of eating animals. Human history is filled with cases where false beliefs about differences between the sexes, people of different races and ethnicities, and humans and nonhumans have led to unjustified ethical beliefs and, thereby, unethical practices such as discrimination, subjugation, slavery and genocide.

Another way in which ethical beliefs can be assessed without appealing to any particular cultural perspective is by evaluating the reasoning that is used in support of them. Ethics, like science, makes use of inferences. In scientific reasoning, there is an inference from the empirical data to the conclusion. Scientific conclusions are justified only if the data is good and the inference is valid. Errors in scientific reasoning occur. For example, sometimes the conclusion drawn is not the best explanation for the data, or a causal relationship is asserted when the data is not robust enough to warrant it. Therefore, part of scientific practice involves assessing the data and reasoning of others to identify when errors occur. The same situation obtains in ethics, where conclusions are established by reasoning from premises—empirical claims, value claims and principles—to conclusions. Sometimes, the inferences made are invalid, and the conclusion does not logically follow from the premises. Therefore, the conclusion is unjustified.

Common errors in reasoning are called fallacies, and several forms of fallacious reasoning are common in food ethics. For example, the *perfectionist fallacy* came up in the discussion about our responsibility to address global malnutrition; the *fallacy of appeal to nature* arose in the discussion of eating animals; the *false dilemma fallacy* arose in the discussion of synthetic meat; and the *fallacy of appeal to the crowd* came up in the discussion of genetically modified animals. Other fallacies that are common in food ethics and policy include the *ad hominem fallacy*—attacking the person who holds a view, rather than discussing the merits of the view—and the *fallacy of hasty conclusion*—making an overall ethical assessment on the basis of only some of the relevant information. Both of these occur frequently in the food system discourse. Thus, another way to evaluate ethical beliefs, in addition to assessing the information on which they are based, is to assess the quality of the reasoning offered in support of them. If the reasoning is fallacious, then the view is not justified by it.

A third method by which it is possible to evaluate ethical beliefs and practices, in a way that does not assume any cultural perspectives, is in terms of internal consistency. If a culture (or a person) endorses ethical claims that are inconsistent with each other, or if they endorse a principle but not its implications, then at least one of the beliefs must be false. For example, if a society or culture regards animal cruelty as wrong (and passes laws against it), but then allows and subsidizes CAFOs in which animals suffer just to satisfy people's food preferences, then their values, laws and practices are inconsistent with each other, and some of them should be revised. Similarly, if a person believes that pain is intrinsically bad, but that animals are not ethically considerable, then their views are in tension with each other, unless there is an ethically relevant difference between humans and nonhuman animals. Thus, another way to evaluate cultural (and individual) ethical beliefs is by the extent to which they are internally coherent.

Taken together, these methods—assessing the factual bases of beliefs, the quality of reasoning in support of them, and their internal consistency and coherence—provide a robust set of resources for evaluating and adjudicating among the ethical beliefs and practices of individuals and cultures. They employ standards of reasoning and empirical information, so do not involve judging one culture's beliefs and practices from the ethical perspective of another culture. Whether animals feel pain is not dependent on cultural context. Inferring from something's occurring in nature to its being permissible for people to do is logically invalid, regardless of one's cultural identity. If this is correct, then ethics is not just a matter of cultural practice, and it is not subjective. It is possible to rigorously evaluate the ethical beliefs, norms and practices of individuals and cultures. Therefore, the challenge of adjudication can be met, and ethical relativism is mistaken.

One response sometimes made to this argument against ethical relativism is that empirical information and standards of reasoning are themselves culturally dependent. However, this seems highly implausible. The amount of deforestation that occurs for agricultural purposes and the robustness of ocean fisheries are objective facts about the state of the world, independent of what anyone or any culture believes about them. If everyone were to believe that the ocean's fisheries are not at all depleted, it would not change the fact that they are in fact severely depleted. Moreover, to infer from the fact that one fishery is not depleted to the conclusion that the world's fisheries are robust is fallacious—it claims more than the evidence warrants—regardless of one's cultural context. It is true that scientific practice is very often culturally influenced with respect to such things as what gets studied, what sort of data is taken as reliable, and what sort of inferences are made. However, these are themselves subject to critical evaluation. As discussed above, sometimes science (and ethics) is not done as well as it ought to be.

Another argument sometimes made in favor of cultural relativism is that we must respect and be tolerant of cultural practices different from our own and that this respect requires that we embrace ethical relativism. However, rather than showing that ethical relativism is true, this argument actually assumes that it is false. If it is true that every culture ought to respect and be tolerant of cultural practices different from its own, then there is nonrelativistic ethical truth—i.e. that every culture should respect every other culture. For this reason, proponents of this argument often move from *global relativism*—i.e. that the truth of *all* ethical claims are culturally relative or subjective—to *selective relativism*—i.e. that the truth of *many* ethical claims are culturally relative.

THE NORMATIVITY OF CULTURE

The discussion above regarding cultural relativism suggested that cultural norms, beliefs and practices are not always definitive when it comes to ethics. The fact that a practice is a cultural tradition or is culturally accepted does not by itself imply that it is permissible to do, since they often can be evaluated as more or less justified. There is a fallacy of appeal to tradition. However, this is not to claim that cultural considerations are not normatively significant at all. As discussed at the start of this chapter, cultural traditions are important to cultural identity, which is valuable, and they can create value. Thus, it is necessary to revisit the question of when and to what extent cultural considerations should be taken as normative in ethics.

In some cases, cultural practices are conventions that set norms for what people ought to do. For example, the fact that people drive on the left side of the road in Australia is a convention. It is a convention because there is no reason why a system of driving on the left side of the road is more justified than one with driving on the right side of the road. But once the convention is set, it becomes normative. The fact that the convention (and law) is left-side driving in Australia implies that everyone driving in Australia ought to do it. Smooth and safe road travel depends upon people adhering to the practice, and knowingly and intentionally violating the convention would be unethical. Many things are cultural or social conventions, from etiquette to family arrangements to what foods are eaten on holidays. Sometimes, as in the case of driving, the conventions become ethically normative—i.e. it is wrong to violate them. In other cases, such as the arrangement of utensils on the table, they are not—it is not unethical to put the fork next to the spoon.

The issue, then, is sorting out when cultural practices are ethically normative and when they are not. The cases discussed above—driving and utensils—suggest that this is tied to the importance of what is at stake. In the case of driving, something valuable is at stake: the well-being of other people. Therefore, not only is it permissible to adhere to the norm, it is obligatory to do so. In utensil etiquette, something minor (if anything) is at stake—perhaps only how others will judge you. Therefore, it is acceptable to violate the norm, even for trivial reasons.

The discussion above concerned when it is permissible to violate a cultural norm. Another type of case is when cultural practices are contrary to other normative considerations. Can the fact that something is part of a cultural tradition make it acceptable if it would otherwise be considered ethically problematic? It seems as if it can sometimes. For example, it is normally not permissible to intentionally frighten children, but it is permissible to do so on Hallowe'en. However, there are limits to this. It should not be done in a way that truly terrifies them or that would be detrimental to them in the long run, for instance. This suggests that ethical considerations (in this case, the well-being of children) circumscribe what is acceptable, even within a tradition or cultural practice.

Foie gras is a traditional Christmas Eve food in France. There is an explanation for the existence of the cultural practice. However, as discussed above, that there is an explanation does not tell us whether it is ethically acceptable. Let us assume for present purposes that animal suffering is ethically significant (this issue is discussed at length in Chapter 3). Force-feeding ducks and geese to fatten their livers causes them to suffer. Suppose that eating foie gras were not a tradition, but only tasted very good, then (assuming animal suffering is ethically significant) it would be unacceptable, since it would involve causing unnecessary suffering and death for a mere culinary preference. How does the fact that eating foie gras on Christmas Eve is a tradition change the situation? For one thing, it means that it is practiced widely over time and place, as well as actively promulgated or passed on. Normally, when something is considered ethically problematic, the more widespread it is the worse it is. So, in this respect, that eating foie gras is a tradition seems to make it more ethically problematic, not less so. However, that it is a tradition also means that it is connected to cultural identity and valued practices. Is this enough to elevate its normative significance from peripheral to serious—to the point where it might plausibly justify causing unnecessary suffering?

Some think not. When a cultural tradition causes unnecessary suffering, it indicates that there is something problematic with the culture (in this case, the cultural attitude toward animals), so it should not be countenanced. That is to say, the fact that a valued part of cultural practice involves causing unnecessary harm tells us something evaluative about the culture; it does not excuse the practice. (Many people make a similar sort of argument regarding forced marriages and female circumcision.) Moreover, when evaluating cultural value claims, it is necessary to determine how crucial the tradition is to cultural identity and practice. Could it be forgone, revised or substituted without loss of significant cultural value? The Makah, for example, argue that their whale hunt is crucial to their cultural identity and practice, and that there is no reasonable alternative to it (e.g. symbolic "hunts" in which there is no taking of life). However, in the case of Christmas Eve foie gras, it seems implausible that French identity, pride and cultural continuity depend upon the continuation of this particular culinary tradition.

The foregoing suggests that whether an appeal to cultural practice should take precedence over other normative (including ethical) considerations in a particular case depends upon: 1. How significant the practice/tradition is to cultural identity and cultural value; 2. How important the ethical considerations are that are compromised by the practice/tradition; 3. The extent to which the ethical considerations are compromised by the cultural practice; and 4. Whether the practice can be modified or substituted without substantial loss of cultural meaning and value.

FOODIE CULTURE

In places where there is food abundance, food is increasingly treated as a source of entertainment. The Food Network now reaches over 100 million homes in the United States and over 50 percent of Americans report that they watch TV shows about cooking "very often" or "occasionally." We are amused by celebrity chefs, engrossed by food competitions, and eager to learn about bizarre foods in exotic places. Eating is also increasingly treated as recreation. As discussed in Chapter 1, people in affluent nations spend a comparatively small percentage of their income on food. Many of us can afford to eat out frequently and can pay to experience more unusual foods, boutique foods, elaborately prepared foods, novel foods and gourmet foods.

Foodie refers to a person who embraces cooking, eating and drinking as a hobby or pursuit. Foodies are invested in cultivating appreciation and knowledge of foods and beverages. They prioritize food aesthetics and experiences in their lives. They seek out novel and elevated gastronomic experiences. They engage in *food tourism* (or *culinary tourism*), traveling to new locations in order to experience exotic or exceptional foods. They develop skill in food preparation. Foodies are people for whom cooking and consuming food are focal practices.

Foodieism is controversial. This might seem surprising. Why should a hobby around food and eating be any more problematic than one around sport or art? If people have excess time and resources, and would like to spend them developing an aesthetic appreciation of artisanal cheese and single malt scotch, learning the history and techniques of North Indian cooking, traveling the wine regions of Europe, or just eating at the latest and most innovative restaurants in town, why should anyone object? Consideration of autonomy should allow for people spending their resources and leisure as they like, so long as it does not involve engaging in anything unethical and does not distract from things that are more important.

Foodieism is often associated with slow foods and local foods, and the objections to it are similar to some made to those aspects of the alternative food movement. For example, foodieism is charged with being elitist and self-serving, since it is centered on spending large amounts of resources on oneself and is accessible only to those who are affluent. It is also thought to be classist, since it valorizes gourmet and boutique foods that appeal to the wealthy while demeaning the fast and processed foods that are favored by the working poor and middle class. It is also seen as distracting from real food problems, such as food insecurity, malnutrition and ecological degradation, and as using aesthetics as a justification for maintaining ethically problematic practices, such as veal and foie gras production and high-emissions diets. Its treatment of unfamiliar foods and peoples as strange and exotic "others" that we can visit and experience is thought to objectify and commodify them and to have vestiges of colonialism and ethnicism.

To some extent, these concerns are raised against a caricature of foodies, or at least to foodieism at its worst. Many people who have a deep aesthetic interest in food, and who take up food-related hobbies or careers, are not selfish, elitist, ecologically insensitive or ethically unaware. As discussed in Chapter 1, Slow Foods has expanded its mission to include food justice, human rights, food access, sustainability and animal welfare in addition to the promotion of food aesthetics and appreciation. (However, concerns have been raised about the depth of those commitments when they come into conflict with culturally significant or gourmet foods.) There are elitist, self-serving and irresponsible foodies and foodie organizations, but there are also small business owners, farmers, teachers and community organizations that are interested in connecting food appreciation to education, nutrition, food security and community uplift. Being committed to food aesthetics leaves open how that interest is pursued. Just as it is possible to be a virtuous or a vicious artist or angler, it is possible to be a virtuous or a vicious foodie. The real question is how to "love food" in compassionate, just and ecologically considerate ways.

CONCLUSION

Culture intersects with food ethics in two ways. First, there are ethical issues and questions raised by cultural traditions and practices—e.g. how to respect them and when to defer to them. Second, there are prescriptive questions about what sort of food culture we ought to aim to develop. However, whether a practice is connected to traditional foodways or to emerging food cultures, the evaluative questions are largely the same: Is it respectful of the autonomy and practices of others? Is it sustainable? Does it promulgate problematic power relationships? Is it accessible and inclusive? Does it strengthen community? Is it compassionate? And does it improve and enrich people's lives?

FURTHER READING

Several of the resources listed at the end of previous chapters address social and ethical issues at the intersection of food and culture:

Food, Culture & Society (Bloomsbury), a journal published by the Association for the Study of Food and Society

Vandana Shiva, *Stolen Harvest: The Hijacking of the Global Food Supply* (South End Press)

Alison Hope Alkon and Julian Agyeman, eds., *Cultivating Food Justice: Race, Class, and Sustainability* (MIT Press)

Robert Gottlieb and Anupama Joshi, *Food Justice* (MIT Press)

Carlo Petrini, *Slow Food: The Case for Taste* (Columbia University Press)

Ted Kerasote, *Bloodties: Nature, Culture, and the Hunt* (Kodansha)

Other excellent resources on the topics discussed in this chapter include:

Lisa Heldke, *Exotic Appetites: Ruminations of a Food Adventurer* (Routledge)

Carolyn Korsmeyer, *The Taste Culture Reader: Experiencing Food and Drink* (Bloomsbury)

E.N. Anderson, *Everyone Eats: Understanding Food and Culture* (New York University Press)

Food and Foodways (Taylor & Francis), a journal that publishes articles on the history and culture of food

Two accessible introductions to ethical relativism and metaethics more generally are:

Russ Shafer-Landau, *Whatever Happened to Good and Evil?* (Oxford University Press)

James Rachels, *The Elements of Moral Philosophy* (McGraw-Hill)

BIBLIOGRAPHY

Alexandratos, N. and Bruinsma, J. 2012, *World Agriculture towards 2030/2050: The 2012 Revision*, Food and Agriculture Organization of the United Nations, Rome.

Aquastat. 2014, *Water Uses*, Food and Agriculture Organization of the United Nations, Rome. Available from: <http://www.fao.org/nr/water/aquastat/water_use/index.stm>. [May 12, 2014].

Beat. 2010, *Facts and Figures: How Many People in the UK Have an Eating Disorder?*, Beat. Available from: <http://www.b-eat.co.uk/about-beat/media-centre/facts-and-figures/>. [April 20, 2014].

Bentham, J. 1907 [1823], *Introduction to the Principles of Morals and Legislation*, 2nd edn., Oxford: Clarendon Press.

BLS. 2014, *Occupational Employment Statistics: Occupational Employment and Wages, May 2013: Combined Food Preparation and Serving Workers, Including Fast Food*, United States Bureau of Labor Statistics. Available from: <http://www.bls.gov/oes/current/oes353021.htm>. [April 21, 2014].

Buzby, J.C. and Hyman, J. 2012, "Total and Per Capita Value of Food Loss in the United States," *Food Policy*, vol. 75, no. 5, pp. 561–70.

Carlson, R. 2014, "The U.S. Bioeconomy in 2012 Reached \$350 Billion in Revenues, or about 2.5% of GDP," *Synthesis*. Available from: <http://www.synthesis.cc/2014/01/the-us-bioeconomy-in-2012.html>. [April 22, 2014].

Cassidy, E.S., West, P.C., Gerber, J.S. and Foley, J.A. 2013, "Redefining Agricultural Yields: From Tonnes to People Nourished per Hectare," *Environmental Research Letters,* vol. 8, no. 034015. Available from: <http://iopscience.iop.org/1748-9326/8/3/034015>. [May 20, 2014].

Catalyst. 2014, "Knowledge Center: Women CEOs of the Fortune 1000," *Catalyst*. Available from: <http://www.catalyst.org/knowledge/women-ceos-fortune-1000>. [April 20, 2014].

CDC. 2011, *Reducing Access to Sugar-sweetened Beverages among Youth*, Centers for Disease Control and Prevention. Available from: <http://www.cdc.gov/features/healthybeverages>. [April 17, 2014].

———. 2013, *Food Allergies in Schools*, Centers for Disease Control and Prevention. Available from: <http://www.cdc.gov/healthyyouth/foodallergies/>. [April 20, 2014].

Chandy, L. and Gertz, G. 2011, *Poverty in Numbers: The Changing State of Global Poverty from 2005 to 2015*, The Brookings Institution, Washington, D.C.

CIA. 2014, *The World Factbook*, Central Intelligence Agency. Available from: <https://www.cia.gov/library/publications/the-world-factbook/rankorder/2127rank.html>. [April 20, 2014].

Cleland, J., Bernstein, S., Ezeh, A., Faundes, A., Glasier, A. and Innis, J. 2006, "Family Planning: The Unfinished Agenda," *The Lancet*, vol. 368, no. 9549, pp. 1810–27.

Costa-Pierce, B.A., Bartley, D.M., Hasan, M., Yusoff, F., Kaushik, S.J., Rana, K., Lemos, D., Bueno, P. and Yakupitiyage, A. 2011, *Responsible Use of Resources for Sustainable Aquaculture*, Global Conference on Aquaculture 2010, Phuket, Thailand, Food and Agriculture Organization of the United Nations, Rome. Available from: <http://ecologicalaquaculture.org/Costa-PierceFAO(2011).pdf>. [May 20, 2014].

DEFRA. 2005, *Managing GM Crops with Herbicides: Effects on Wildlife*, Department for Environment, Food and Rural Affairs, York.

———. 2012, *Food Statistics Pocketbook: 2012 – in year update*, Department for Environment, Food and Rural Affairs, York.

Department of Labor. 2014, *Data and Statistics*, United States Department of Labor. Available from: <http://www.dol.gov/wb/stats/stats_data.htm>. [May 16, 2014].

De Schutter, O. 2011, *Agroecology and the Right to Food*, Report presented to the 16th Session of the United Nations Human Rights Council. Available from: < http://www.srfood.org/images/stories/pdf/officialreports/20110308_a-hrc-16-49_agroecology_en.pdf>. [May 12, 2014].

DeSilver, D. 2013, "Obesity and Poverty Don't Always Go Together," *Fact Tank*. Available from: <http://www.pewresearch.org/fact-tank/2013/11/13/obesity-and-poverty-dont-always-go-together/>. [April 20, 2014].

Dhar, Tirtha and Baylis, Kathy. 2011, "Fast Food Consumption and the Ban on Advertising Targeting Children: The Québec Experience," *Journal of Marketing Research,* vol. 48, no. 5, pp. 799–813.

DSB. 2011, *Trends and Implications of Climate Change for National and International Security*, United States Department of Defense, Defense Science Board, Washington, D.C.

EEOC. 2014a, *Sexual Harassment Charges: EEOC & FEPAs Combined: FY 1997–FY 2011*, U.S. Equal Employment Opportunity Commission. Available from: <http://www.eeoc.gov/eeoc/statistics/enforcement/sexual_harassment.cfm>. [April 20, 2014].

——. 2014b, *Enforcement and Litigation Statistics*, U.S. Equal Employment Opportunity Commission. Available from: <http://www.eeoc.gov/eeoc/statistics/enforcement/index.cfm>. [April 20, 2014].

EPA. 2011, *What's the Problem?*, United States Environmental Protection Agency. Available from: <http://www.epa.gov/region9/animalwaste/problem.html>. [July 1, 2014].

——. 2014a, *Concentrated Animal Feeding Operations (CAFOs): What is a CAFO?*, United States Environmental Protection Agency. Available from: <http://www.epa.gov/region7/water/cafo/>. [April 20, 2014].

——. 2014b, *Estimated Animal Agriculture Nitrogen and Phosphorus from Manure*, United States Environmental Protection Agency. Available from: <http://www2.epa.gov/nutrient-policy-data/estimated-animal-agriculture-nitrogen-and-phosphorus-manure>. [April 20, 2014].

Ezeh, A., Bongaarts, J. and Mberu, B. 2012, "Global Population Trends and Policy Options," *The Lancet*, vol. 380, no. 9837, pp. 142–48.

FAO. 2004, *The State of Food and Agriculture, Agricultural Biotechnology: Meeting the Needs of the Poor?*, Food and Agriculture Organization of the United Nations, Rome.

——. 2006, *Livestock's Long Shadow: Environmental Issues and Options*, Food and Agriculture Organization of the United Nations, Rome.

——. 2010, "World Deforestation Decreases, but Remains Alarming in Many Countries," Food and Agriculture Organization of the United Nations. Available from: <http://www.fao.org/news/story/en/item/40893/icode/>. [April 20, 2014].

——. 2011, *The State of Food Insecurity in the World: How Does International Price Volatility Affect Domestic Economies and Food Security?*, Food and Agriculture Organization of the United Nations, Rome.

——. 2012a, *The State of World Fisheries and Aquaculture 2012*, Food and Agriculture Organization of the United Nations, Rome.

——. 2012b, *The State of Food Insecurity in the World: Economic Growth Is Necessary but not Sufficient to Accelerate Reduction of Hunger and Malnutrition*, Food and Agriculture Organization of the United Nations, Rome.

——. 2013a, *Food Wastage Footprint: Impacts on Natural Resources – Summary Report*, Food and Agriculture Organization of the United Nations, Rome.

——. 2013b, *The State of the World's Land and Water Resources for Food and Agriculture (SOLAW): Managing Systems at Risk*, Food and Agriculture Organization of the United Nations, Rome.

——. 2013c, *The State of Food Insecurity in the World: The Multiple Dimensions of Food Security*, Food and Agriculture Organization of the United Nations, Rome.

——. 2014a, "Greenhouse Gas Emissions from Agriculture, Forestry and Other Land Use," Food and Agriculture Organization of the United Nations. Available from: <http://www.fao.org/resources/infographics/infographics-details/en/c/218650/>. [April 4, 2014].

——. 2014b, *Common Oceans: Global Sustainable Fisheries Management and Biodiversity Conservation in Areas beyond National Jurisdiction*, Food and Agriculture Organization of the United Nations. Available from: <http://www.fao.org/docrep/019/i2943e/i2943e.pdf?utm_source=twitter&utm_medium=social+media&utm_campaign = faoknowledge>. [May 17, 2014].

FAOSTAT. 2008a, *FAO Methodology for the Measurement of Food Deprivation: Updating the Minimum Dietary Energy Requirements*. Food and Agriculture Organization of the United Nations Statistics Division, Rome.

——. 2008b, *FAOSTAT*, Food and Agriculture Organization of the United Nations Statistics Division. Available from: <http://faostat.fao.org>. [August 31, 2010].

——. 2010, "Minimum Dietary Energy Requirement," Food and Agriculture Organization of the United Nations Statistics Division. Available from: <http://www.fao.org/fileadmin/templates/ess/documents/food_security_statistics/MinimumDietaryEnergyRequirement_en.xls>. [May 12, 2014].

——. 2013, *FAO Statistical Yearbook: 2013: World Food and Agriculture*, Food and Agriculture Organization of the United Nations Statistics Division, Rome.

——. 2014a, *FAOSTAT*, Food and Agriculture Organization of the United Nations Statistics Division. Available from: <http://faostat.fao.org/>. [April 21, 2014].

——. 2014b, *Agriculture, Forestry and Other Land Use Emissions by Sources and Removals by Sinks: 1990–2011 Analysis*, Food and Agriculture Organization of the United Nations Statistics Division. Available from: <http://www.fao.org/docrep/019/i3671e/i3671e.pdf>. [May 20, 2014].

Fernandez-Cornejo, J. and McBride, W. 2000, *Genetically Engineered Crops for Pest Management in US Agriculture: Farm-Level Effects*, United States Department of Agriculture, Economic Research Service, Report no. 786.

Foley, J.A., Ramankutty, N., Brauman, K.A., Cassidy, E.S., Gerber, J.S. and Johnston, M. 2011, "Solutions for a Cultivated Planet," *Nature*, vol. 478, no. 7369, pp. 337–42.

FSA. 2011, *Foodborne Disease Strategy: 2010–15: An FSA Programme for the Reduction of Foodborne Disease in the UK*, Food Standards Agency, London.

Godfray, H.C.J., Beddington, J.R., Crute, I.R., Haddad, L., Lawrenc, D. and Muir, J.F. 2010, "Food Security: The Challenge of Feeding 9 Billion People," *Science*, vol. 327, no. 5967, pp. 812–18.

Gunders, D. 2012, *Wasted: How America Is Losing Up to 40 Percent of Its Food from Farm to Fork to Landfill*, Natural Resources Defense Council. Available from: <http://www.nrdc.org/food/files/wasted-food-ip.pdf>. [May 20, 2014].

Haberl, H., Erb, K.H., Krausmann, F., Gaube, V., Bondeau, A. and Plutzar, C. 2007, "Quantifying and Mapping the Human Appropriation of Net Primary Production in Earth's Terrestrial Ecosystems," *PNAS*, vol. 104, no. 31, pp. 12942–47.

IPCC. 2007, *Fourth Assessment Report*, Intergovernmental Panel on Climate Change, Geneva, UNEP/WMO.

——. 2014, *Fifth Assessment Report*, Intergovernmental Panel on Climate Change, Geneva, UNEP/WMO.

IUCN. 2014, "A Quarter of Sharks and Rays Threatened with Extinction," International Union for Conservation of Nature. Available from: <http://www.iucn.org/?14311/A-quarter-of-sharks-and-rays-threatened-with-extinction>. [April 22, 2014].

James, C. 2013, "ISAAA Report on Global Status of Commercialized Biotech/GM Crops," ISAAA Brief No. 46, ISAAA. Available from: <http://www.isaaa.org/resources/publications/briefs/46/default.asp>. [May 20, 2014].

Krausmann, F., Erb, K.H., Gingrich, S., Haberl, H., Bondeau, A. and Gaube, V. 2013, "Global Human Appropriation of Net Primary Production Doubled in the 20th Century," *PNAS*, vol. 110, no. 25, pp. 10324–29.

Kroll, L. 2014, "Inside the 2014 Forbes Billionaires List: Facts and Figures," *Forbes*. Available from: <http://www.forbes.com/sites/luisakroll/2014/03/03/inside-the-2014-forbes-billionaires-list-facts-and-figures/>. [May 15, 2014].

The Lancet. 2011, "Obesity," *The Lancet*. Available from: <http://www.thelancet.com/series/obesity>. [April 20, 2014].

Love, P. 2010, "Fueling Hunger? Biofuel Grain 'Could Feed 330 Million'," *OECD Insights*. Available from: <http://oecdinsights.org/2010/01/25/biofuel/>. [April 17, 2014].

MacDonald, J. and McBride, W. 2009, "The Transformation of U.S. Livestock Agriculture: Scale, Efficiency, and Risks," *United States Department of Agriculture, Economic Research Service*. Available from: <http://www.ers.usda.gov/publications/eib-economic-information-bulletin/eib43.aspx>. [April 20, 2014].

Mendes, E. 2012, "Fewer Americans Have Employer-Based Health Insurance: Medicare, Medicaid, or Military/Veterans' Benefits Covers 25.2%," *Gallup*. Available from: <http://www.gallup.com/poll/152621/fewer-americans-employer-based-health-insurance.aspx>. [April 22, 2014].

Milanovic, B. 2012, *The Haves and the Have-Nots: A Brief and Idiosyncratic History of Global Inequality*, New York: Basic Books.

Mueller, N.D., Gerber, J.S., Johnston, M., Ray, D.K., Ramankutty, N. and Foley, J.A. 2012, "Closing Yield Gaps through Nutrient and Water Management," *Nature*, vol. 490, no. 7419, pp. 254–57.

Myrskyla, M., Kohler, H.P. and Billari, F.C. 2009, "Advances in Development Reverse Fertility Declines," *Nature*, vol. 460, no. 7256, pp. 741–43.

NAWS. 2004, *The National Agricultural Workers Survey*, United States Department of Labor, Employment and Training Administration. Available from: <http://www.doleta.gov/agworker/report9/toc.cfm>. [April 21, 2014].

Nicolia, A., Manzo, A., Veronesi, F. and Rosellini, D. 2013, "An Overview of the Last 10 Years of Genetically Engineered Crop Safety Research," *Critical Reviews in Biotechnology*. Available from: <http://www.geneticliteracyproject.org/wp/wp-content/uploads/2013/10/Nicolia-20131.pdf>. [April 20, 2014].

Nielsen. 2012, "Fifty Nine Percent of Consumers around the World Indicate Difficulty Understanding Nutritional Labels," Nielsen. Available from: <http://www.nielsen.com/us/en/press-room/2012/fifty-nine-percent-of-consumers-around-the-world-indicate-diffic.html>. [April 22, 2014].

NIMH. 2014, *Health & Education: Statistics*, National Institute of Mental Health. Available from: <http://www.nimh.nih.gov/statistics/index.shtml>. [April 20, 2014].

NOAA. 2012, *Status of Stocks 2012: Annual Report to Congress on the Status of U.S. Fisheries*, National Oceanic and Atmospheric Administration, Fisheries. Available from: <http://www.nmfs.noaa.gov/sfa/statusoffisheries/2012/2012_SOS_RTC.pdf>. [May 20, 2014].

——. 2013, *Wild-Caught Seafood*, National Oceanic and Atmospheric Administration, Fish Watch. Available from: <http://www.fishwatch.gov/wild_seafood/>. [April 21, 2014].

OECD. 2013a, "Aid to Poor Countries Slips Further as Governments Tighten Budgets," *Organization for Economic Cooperation and Development*. Available from: <http://www.oecd.org/newsroom/aidtopoorcountriesslipsfurtheras governmentstightenbudgets.htm>. [April 20, 2014].

——. 2013b, *OECD Compendium of Agri-environmental Indicators, Organization for Economic Cooperation and Development*. Available from: <http://www.oecd-ilibrary.org/agriculture-and-food/oecd-compendium-of-agri-environmental-indicators_9789264186217-en>. [April 21, 2014].

Ogden, C.L., Kit, B.K., Carroll, M.D. and Park, S. 2011, "Consumption of Sugar Drinks in the United States, 2005–2008," Centers for Disease Control and Prevention, *NCHS Data Brief*, no. 71. Available from: <http://www.cdc.gov/nchs/data/databriefs/db71.htm>. [May 20, 2014].

Ogden, C.L., Carroll, M.D., Kit, B.K. and Flegal, K.M. 2012, "Prevalence of Obesity and Trends in Body Mass Index Among US Children and Adolescents, 1999–2010," *The Journal of the American Medical Association*, vol. 307, no. 5, pp. 483–90.

——. 2013, "Prevalence of Obesity among Adults: United States, 2011–2012," Centers for Disease Control and Prevention, *NCHS Data Brief*, no. 131. Available from: <http://www.cdc.gov/nchs/data/databriefs/db131.htm>. [May 20, 2014].

Olinto, P., Beegle, K., Sobrado, C. and Uematsu, H. 2013, "The State of the Poor: Where Are the Poor, Where is Extreme Poverty Harder to End, and What Is the Current Profile of the World's Poor?," World Bank, *Economic Premise*, no. 125. Available from: <http://siteresources.worldbank.org/EXTPREMNET/Resources/EP125.pdf>. [May 20, 2014].

Ortiz, I. and Cummins, M. 2011, *Global Inequality: Beyond the Bottom Billion – A Rapid Review of Income Distribution in 141 Countries*, UNICEF, Social Inclusion, Policy and Budgeting. Available from: <http://www.unicef.org/socialpolicy/index_58230.html>. [May 20, 2014].

O'Sullivan, M. and Kersley, R. 2012, "The Global Wealth Pyramid," Credit Suisse, *Global Trends*. Available from: <https://www.credit-suisse.com/us/en/news-and-expertise/news/economy/global-trends.article.html/article/pwp/news-and-expertise/2012/10/en/the-global-wealth-pyramid.html>. [April 17, 2014].

Pirog, R. and Benjamin, A. 2005, *Calculating Food Miles for a Multiple Ingredient Food Product*, Leopold Center for Sustainable Agriculture. Available from: <http://www.leopold.iastate.edu/pubs-and-papers/2005-03-calculating-food-miles>. [April 20, 2014].

Powell, L.M., Schermbeck, R.M., and Chaloupka, F.J. 2013, "Nutritional Content of Food and Beverage Products in Television Advertisements Seen on Children's Programming," *Childhood Obesity*, vol. 9, no. 6, pp. 524–31.

Pretty, J. and Hine, R. 2001, *Reducing Food Poverty with Sustainable Agriculture: A Summary of New Evidence*, University of Essex, Centre for Environment and Society. Available from: <http://siteresources.worldbank.org/INTPESTMGMT/General/20380457/ReduceFoodPovertywithSustAg.pdf>. [May 20, 2014].

Pretty, J.N., Morison, J.I.L. and Hine, R.E. 2003, "Reducing Food Poverty by Increasing Agricultural Sustainability in Developing Countries," *Agriculture, Ecosystems & Environment*, vol. 95, no. 1, pp. 217–34.

Pretty, J.N., Noble, A.D., Bossio, D., Dixon, J., Hine, R.E. and Penning de Vries, F.W.T. 2006, "Resource-Conserving Agriculture Increases Yields in Developing Countries," *Environmental Science & Technology*, vol. 40, no. 4, pp. 1114–19.

Rao, M., Afshin, A., Singh, G., and Mozaffarian, D. 2013, "Do Healthier Foods and Diet Patterns Cost more than Less Healthy Options? A Systematic Review and Meta-analysis," *BMJ Open*, vol. 3, no. 12, e004277. Available from: <http://bmjopen.bmj.com/content/3/12/e004277.full.pdf+html>. [April 21, 2014].

Reading, B.F. 2011, "Education Leads to Lower Fertility and Increased Prosperity," Earth Policy Institute, *Data Highlights*. Available from: <http://www.earth-policy.org/data_highlights/2011/highlights13>. [May 12, 2014].

Robert Half. 2014, "More than a Third of UK Female Employees Have Faced Barriers During Their Career, While Half of HR Directors Believe Progress is Being Made," Robert Half. Available from: <http://www.roberthalf.co.uk/id/PR-03852/women-still-facing-gender-barriers-in-uk-business>. [May 15, 2014].

Running, S.W. 2012, "A Measurable Planetary Boundary for the Biosphere," *Science*, vol. 337, no. 6101, pp. 1458–59.

Schmitt, J. and Jones, J. 2013, "Slow Progress for Fast-Food Workers," Center for Economic and Policy Research. Available from: <http://www.cepr.net/index.php/blogs/cepr-blog/slow-progress-for-fast-food-workers>. [April 21, 2014].

Seufert, V., Ramankutty, N. and Foley, J.A. 2012, "Comparing the Yields of Organic and Conventional Agriculture," *Nature*, vol. 485, no. 7397, pp. 229–32.

Smith-Spangler, C., Brandeau, M.L., Hunter, G.E., Bavinger, J.C., Pearson, M. and Eschbach, P.J. 2012, "Are Organic Foods Safer or Healthier than Conventional Alternatives? A Systematic Review," *Annals of Internal Medicine*, vol. 157, no. 5, pp. 348–66.

Swinburn, B.A., Sacks, G., Hall, K.D., McPherson, K., Finegood, D.T. and Moodie, M.L. 2011, "The Global Obesity Pandemic: Shaped By Global Drivers and Local Environments," *The Lancet*, vol. 378, no. 9793, pp. 804–14.

Thomas, C.D., Cameron, A., Green, R.E., Bakkenes, M., Beaumont, L.J. and Collingham, Y.C. 2004, "Extinction Risk from Climate Change," *Nature*, vol. 427, no. 6970, pp. 145–48.

UN. 1948, *Universal Declaration of Human Rights*, United Nations, Office of the High Commissioner for Human Rights. Available from: <http://www.ohchr.org/en/udhr/pages/introduction.aspx>. [April 20, 2014].

——. 1966, *International Covenant on Economic, Social and Cultural Rights*, United Nations, Office of the High Commissioner for Human Rights. Available from: <http://www.ohchr.org/EN/ProfessionalInterest/Pages/CESCR.aspx>. [April 20, 2014].

——. 2009, *World Population Prospects: The 2008 Revision, Highlights*, United Nations, Department of Economic and Social Affairs, New York.

——. 2013a, *World Population Prospects: The 2012 Revision, Highlights and Advance Tables*, United Nations, Department of Economic and Social Affairs, New York.

——. 2013b, *The Millennium Development Goals Report 2013*, United Nations, New York.

UNICEF. 2011, *Statistics By Area/Child Nutrition*, UNICEF, Childinfo. Available from: <http://data.unicef.org/nutrition/malnutrition>. [April 20, 2014].

——. 2013a, *Water, Sanitation and Hygiene*, UNICEF. Available from: <http://www.unicef.org/wash/>. [April 22, 2014].

——. 2013b, *Levels & Trends in Child Mortality: Report 2013*, UNICEF, WHO and World Bank. Available from: <http://www.childinfo.org/files/ Child_Mortality_Report_2013.pdf>. [May 15, 2014].

USDA. 2012a, "U.S. Agricultural Trade: Import Share of Consumption," United States Department of Agriculture, Economic Research Service. Available from: <http://www.ers.usda.gov/topics/international-markets-trade/us-agricultural-trade/import-share-of-consumption.aspx#.U02Wdq2wL4P>. [April 21, 2014].

——. 2012b, "Dairy: Background," United States Department of Agriculture, Economic Research Service. Available from: <http://www.ers.usda.gov/ topics/animal-products/dairy/background.aspx#.Utdh32RDuFA>. [April 20, 2014].

——. 2013a, "Fertilizer Use and Price," United States Department of Agriculture, Economic Research Service. Available from: <http://www.ers. usda.gov/data-products/fertilizer-use-and-price.aspx>. [April 20, 2014].

——. 2013b, "Irrigation & Water Use," United States Department of Agriculture, Economic Research Service. Available from: <http://www.ers.usda.gov/topics/ farm-practices-management/irrigation-water-use.aspx#.Uo5QFWR4bsg>. [April 20, 2014].

——. 2013c, "Farmers Markets and Local Food Marketing," United States Department of Agriculture, Agricultural Marketing Service. Available from: <http://www.ams.usda.gov/AMSv1.0/farmersmarkets>. [May 12, 2014].

——. 2014a, "Food Expenditures: Overview," United States Department of Agriculture, Economic Research Service. Available from: <http://www.ers. usda.gov/data-products/food-expenditures.aspx#26654>. [April 20, 2014].

——. 2014b, "Corn: Background," United States Department of Agriculture, Economic Research Service. Available from: <http://www.ers.usda.gov/ topics/crops/corn/background.aspx#.UmfYw5R4bsg>. [April 20, 2014].

——. 2014c, "Food Security in the U.S.," United States Department of Agriculture, Economic Research Service. Available from: <http://www.ers.usda.gov/topics/ food-nutrition-assistance/food-security-in-the-us.aspx#.U3PhnIFdVyz>. [May 14, 2014].

USDA-NASS. 2014, "Milk: Production per Cow by Year, US," United States Department of Agriculture/National Agricultural Statistics Service. Available from: <http://www.nass.usda.gov/Charts_and_Maps/Milk_Production_and_ Milk_Cows/cowrates.asp>. [April 20, 2014].

USFWS. 2012, *2011 National Survey of Fishing, Hunting, and Wildlife-Associated Recreation State Overview*, United States Fish and Wildlife Service. Available from: <http://digitalmedia.fws.gov/cdm/ref/collection/document/id/858>. [May 20, 2014].

Van Huis, A., Van Itterbeeck, J., Klunder, H., Mertens, E., Halloran, A., and Muir, G. 2013, *Edible Insects: Future Prospects for Food and Feed Security*, Food and Agriculture Organization of the United Nations. Available from: <http://www.fao.org/docrep/018/i3253e/i3253e.pdf>. [May 20, 2014].

Wang, Y.C., McPherson, K., Marsh, T., Gortmaker, S.L. and Brown, M. 2011, "Health and Economic Burden of the Projected Obesity Trends in the USA and the UK," *The Lancet*, vol. 378, no. 9793, pp. 815–25.

Weber, C.L. and Matthews, H.S. 2008, "Food-Miles and the Relative Climate Impacts of Food Choices in the United States," *Environmental Science & Technology*, vol. 42, no. 10, pp. 3508–13.

WHO. 2013, "Obesity and Overweight," World Health Organization. Available from: <http://www.who.int/mediacentre/factsheets/fs311/en/index.html>. [April 17, 2014].

——. 2014, "Water Sanitation Health," World Health Organization. Available from: <http://www.who.int/water_sanitation_health/en/>. [April 17, 2014].

World Bank. 2011, *World Development Report 2012: Gender Equality and Development*, The International Bank for Reconstruction and Development/ The World Bank, Washington, D.C.

——. 2013, "Migrants from Developing Countries to Send Home $414 Billion in Earnings in 2013," World Bank. Available from: <http://www.worldbank. org/en/news/feature/2013/10/02/Migrants-from-developing-countries-to-send-home-414-billion-in-earnings-in-2013>. [April 20, 2014].

——. 2014a, "Data: Agricultural Land (% of Land Area)," World Bank. Available from: <http://data.worldbank.org/indicator/AG.LND.AGRI.ZS? order=wbapi_data_value_2011+wbapi_data_value+wbapi_data_value-last& sort=asc>. [April 8, 2014].

——. 2014b, "Data: Proportion of Seats Held By Women in National Parliaments (%)," World Bank. Available from: <http://data.worldbank. org/indicator/SG.GEN.PARL.ZS>. [April 17, 2014].

——. 2014c, "Data: GDP Ranking," World Bank. Available from: <http:// data.worldbank.org/data-catalog/GDP-ranking-table>. [April 20, 2014].

World Food Programme. 2012, "How High Food Prices Affect The World's Poor," World Food Programme. Available from: <http://www.wfp.org/ stories/how-high-food-prices-affect-worlds-poor>. [April 17, 2014].

World Watch Institute. 2004, *State of the World 2004: Special Focus, The Consumer Society*, New York: Norton.

——. 2012, "Despite Drop from 2009 Peak, Agricultural Land Grabs Still Remain Above Pre-2005 Levels," World Watch Institute, *Vital Signs Online*. Available from: <http://www.worldwatch.org/despite-drop-2009-peak-agricultural-land-grabs-still-remain-above-pre-2005-levels>. [April 23, 2014].

Worm, B., Barbier, E.B., Beaumont, B., Duffy, J.E., Folke, C. and Halpern, B.S. 2006, "Impacts of Biodiversity Loss on Ocean Ecosystem Services," *Science*, vol. 314, no. 5800, pp. 787–90.

INDEX

9 780415 836449